DATE DUE

Return Material Promptly

CAREERS FOR

BORN LEADERS

& Other Decisive Types

CAREERS FOR

BORN LEADERS

& Other
Decisive Types

Blythe Camenson

VGM Career Horizons

NTC/Contemporary Publishing Group

Library of Congress Cataloging-in-Publication Data

Camenson, Blythe.
    Careers for born leaders & other decisive types / Blythe Camenson.
        p. cm. -- (VGM careers for you series)
    ISBN 0-8442-2292-5 (cloth). -- ISBN 0-8442-2293-3 (pbk.)
    1. Executives--Vocational guidance. 2. Career development.
    3. Executive ability. 4. Leadership. I. Title. II. Series.
    HD38.2.C358 1998
    658.4'0023'73--dc21   97-50253
                                                                                    CIP

Published by VGM Career Horizons
An imprint of NTC/Contemporary Publishing Group, Inc.
4255 West Touhy Avenue, Lincolnwood (Chicago), Illinois 60646-1975 U.S.A.
Copyright © 1998 by NTC/Contemporary Publishing Group, Inc.
Printed in the United States of America.
International Standard Book Number 0-8442-2292-5 (cloth)
                                                             0-8442-2293-3 (paper)
 15   14   13   12   11   10   9   8   7   6   5   4   3   2   1

Contents

Acknowledgments

T he author would like to thank the following born leaders for providing information about their careers:

Julie Benthal, Vice President, Nursing Administration

Diane Camerlo, In-House Counsel, Federal Reserve Bank

LeAnne Coury, Assistant Director, Sales

Laurie DeJong, Assistant Director, Physical Therapy

Linda Dickinson, Chef, Restaurant Co-Owner

Chris Fuller, General Manager, Marketing and Sales

Jonas Martin Frost, U.S. Representative

Larry Morin, Senior Vice President, Customer Relations

Laura Murray, School Superintendent

George Ragsdale, Vice President/Engineering Manager

Missy Soleau, Food and Beverage Manager

Ernie Stetenfeld, Director, Public Relations

Kevin Whelan, Marketing/Product Manager

CHAPTER ONE

Examining the Options

Y ou're a leader, not a follower; you're the driver, not a passenger. And though you know reaching the top rung on the ladder might take years of work, you're willing to prepare yourself for that climb.

No matter the setting—financial institutions, the government, corporations, educational facilities, or scores of others—there are certain skills and qualifications you'll need to get to the top. *Careers for Born Leaders* will give you a glance at what it's like in a leadership role and tell you how to get there.

What Makes a Born Leader

Effective executives, administrators, managers, and others in supervisory roles might come from a variety of backgrounds with different experiences and personalities, but they all share some similar attributes.

Persons interested in becoming general managers and top executives must have highly developed personal skills. An analytical mind able to quickly assess large amounts of information and data is also very important. Add to the list the ability to consider and evaluate the interrelationships of numerous factors and to select the best course of action. In the absence of sufficient information, sound intuitive judgment is crucial to reaching favorable decisions. General managers and top executives also must be able to communicate clearly and persuasively with customers, subordinates, and other managers in their firms. They must be confident, motivated, able to motivate others, decisive, and—probably most important—flexible.

Jobs for Born Leaders

General managers and top executives hold more than three million jobs in the United States and Canada. They are found in government and in every industry imaginable. The wholesale and retail trade and services industries employ over six out of ten general managers and top executives.

Senators and representatives, chief executive officers, executive vice presidents for marketing, corporate in-house counsel, department store managers, financial institution vice presidents, brokerage office managers, college deans, school superintendents, hospital administrators, and fire chiefs are examples of general managers and top executives who, at the upper end of the management hierarchy, formulate the policies and direct the operations of the nation's private firms and government agencies.

Most general manager and top executive positions are filled by promoting experienced, lower-level managers. Some companies prefer that their top executives have specialized backgrounds—in finance or marketing, for example. In small firms, where the number of positions is limited, advancement to a higher management position may come slowly. In large firms, promotions may occur more quickly.

General managers may advance to top executive positions, such as executive or administrative vice president, in their own firms or to corresponding general manager positions in larger firms. Similarly, top-level managers may advance to the peak corporate positions of chief operating officer and, finally, chief executive officer. Chief executive officers and other top executives may also become members of the board of directors of one or more firms. Some general managers and top executives with sufficient capital and experience establish their own firms or become independent consultants.

You can accelerate your chances for advancement by participating in company training programs to broaden your knowledge of company policy and operations. Attendance at national or local training programs sponsored by numerous industry and trade associations and continuing education in colleges and universities, normally at company expense, can familiarize managers with the latest developments in management techniques.

Every year, thousands of senior managers, who often have some experience in a particular field such as accounting, engineering, or science, attend executive development programs to facilitate their promotion from functional specialists to general managers. In addition, participation in interdisciplinary conferences and seminars can expand knowledge of national and international issues influencing the managers' firms.

Born Leaders on the Job

The fundamental objective of private organizations is to maintain efficiency and profitability in the face of shifting consumer tastes and needs, accelerating technological complexity, economic interdependence, and domestic and foreign competition. Similarly, nonprofit organizations and government agencies must effectively implement programs subject to budgetary constraints and shifting public preferences. General managers and top executives try to ensure that their organizations meet these objectives.

An organization's general goals and policies are established by the chief executive officer in collaboration with other top executives, usually executive vice presidents, and often with a board of directors. In a large corporation, a chief executive officer may frequently meet with top executives of other corporations, domestic or foreign governments, or outside consultants to discuss matters affecting the organization's policies. Although the chief executive officer retains ultimate authority and responsibility, the chief operating officer may be delegated the authority to oversee executive vice presidents who direct the activities of various departments and are responsible for implementing the organization's policies in these departments.

The scope of executive vice presidents' responsibility depends greatly upon the size of the organization. In large corporations, their duties may be highly specialized. For example, they may oversee general managers of marketing, sales promotion, purchasing, finance, personnel, training, industrial relations, administrative services, electronic data processing, property management, transportation, or legal services departments. In smaller firms, an executive vice president might be responsible for a number of these departments.

General managers, in turn, direct their individual department's activities within the framework of the organization's overall plan. With the help of supervisory managers and their staffs, general managers oversee and strive to motivate workers to achieve their department's goals as rapidly and economically as possible. In smaller organizations, such as independent retail stores or small manufacturers, a general manager may be responsible for purchasing, hiring, training, quality control, and all other day-to-day supervisory duties.

General managers in large firms or government agencies are provided with offices close to the departments they direct and to the top executives to whom they report. Top executives may be provided with spacious offices. Long hours, including evenings and weekends, are the rule for most top executives and general managers, though their schedules may be flexible.

Though still uncommon, more executives are accepting temporary positions, sometimes only working for the duration of one project or several months.

Substantial travel is often required. General managers may travel between national, regional, and local offices to monitor operations and meet with other executives. Top executives may travel to meet with their counterparts in other corporations in the country or overseas. Many attend meetings and conferences that are sponsored by industries and associations and provide invaluable opportunities to meet with peers and keep abreast of technological and other developments. Perks such as reimbursement of an accompanying spouse's travel expenses may help executives cope with frequent or extended periods away from home.

In large corporations, job transfers between the parent company and its local offices or subsidiaries, here or abroad, are common. With increasing domestic and international competition, general managers and top executives are under intense pressure to attain, for example, ever higher production and marketing goals. Executives in charge of poorly performing companies or departments often find that their jobs are in jeopardy.

Training for Born Leaders

The educational background of managers and top executives varies as widely as the nature of their diverse responsibilities. Many general managers and top executives have bachelor's degrees in liberal arts or business administration. Their majors often are related to the departments they direct—for example, accounting for a general manager of finance or computer science for a general manager of information systems.

Graduate and professional degrees are common among top executives. Many managers in administrative, marketing, financial, and manufacturing activities have master's degrees in business administration. Managers in highly technical manufacturing and research activities often have master's or doctoral degrees in engineering or scientific disciplines.

Law degrees are mandatory for general managers of corporate legal departments, and hospital administrators generally have master's degrees in health services administration or business administration. College presidents and school superintendents generally have doctorates, often in education administration; some have law degrees. On the other hand, in some industries, such as retail trade, competent individuals without college degrees may become general managers.

Many general managers in the public sector have liberal arts degrees in public administration or in one of the social sciences, such as economics, psychology, sociology, or urban studies. For others, experience is still the primary qualification. For park superintendents, liberal arts degrees also provide suitable background. Police and fire chiefs are graduates of their respective academies, and degrees in police or fire science or related fields are increasingly important.

The Road Ahead

Employment of general managers and top executives is expected to grow more slowly than the average for all occupations through the year 2005 as companies restructure managerial hierarchies in an effort to cut costs. General managers and top executives may be more affected by these cost-cutting strategies than in the past, thus moderating employment growth.

Although this is a large field, and many openings will occur each year as executives transfer to other positions, start their own businesses, or retire, competition for top managerial jobs will be keen. Many executives who leave their jobs transfer to other executive or managerial positions, limiting openings for new entrants, and large numbers of layoffs resulting from downsizing and restructuring will lead to an ample supply of competent managers. Moreover, the aging of the workforce will result in more senior middle managers vying for a limited number of top executive positions.

Projected employment growth of general managers and top executives varies widely among industries. For example, employment growth is expected to be faster than average in all services industries combined but slower than average in all finance, insurance, and real estate industries. Employment of general managers and top executives is projected to decline in manufacturing industries overall.

Managers whose accomplishments reflect strong leadership qualities and the ability to improve the efficiency or competitive positions of their organizations will have the best opportunities in all industries. In an increasingly global economy, certain types of experience, such as international economics, marketing, or information systems, or knowledge of several disciplines, will also be advantageous.

Top Salaries for Born Leaders

General managers and top executives are among the highest paid workers in the nation. However, salary levels vary substantially depending upon the level of managerial responsibility and length of service as well as the type, size, and location of the firm.

At the highest level, chief executive officers (CEOs) are extremely well paid. According to various surveys, CEOs at top companies can average more than three million dollars annually—including bonuses and stock awards, which are often tied to performance. Salaries are related to the size of the corporation. A top manager in a very large corporation can earn significantly more than a counterpart in a small firm.

Salaries also vary substantially by industry and by type and level of responsibility. Senior vice presidents of lending in banks with $1 billion and higher in assets earned about $200,000 in 1995. The average base salary for top human resources managers was about $136,000. Upper-level computer network managers—including chief information officers, vice presidents, and directors—averaged $83,900. Midlevel managers—including network, data communications, telecommunications, and technical support managers—averaged $59,400. Among top network managers, those in the health care industry were the highest paid, averaging $142,500, while those in wholesale and retail trade were the lowest paid, averaging $56,000. In other industries, top network managers in manufacturing, finance, and utilities were among the highest paid, while those in education and government were among the lowest paid.

Company-paid insurance premiums, physical examinations, executive dining rooms, use of company cars, paid country club memberships, and expense allowances are among the benefits some general managers and top executives in private industry enjoy.

CHAPTER TWO

Government Bigwigs

G o to school. Pay your taxes. Register for the draft. Stop at the stop sign. It seems as though the government is always telling us what to do. Who, then, tells the government what to do? Chief executives and legislators at the federal, state, and local levels do the telling. They are elected or appointed officials who strive to meet the needs of their constituents with an effective and efficient government.

Chief executives are officials who run governmental units that help formulate, carry out, and enforce laws. These officials include the president and vice president of the United States, senators and representatives, state governors and lieutenant governors, county executives, town and township officials, mayors, and managers of cities, counties, towns, and townships. All are elected officials, except local government managers, who are appointed by the local government council or commission.

Government chief executives, such as corporation presidents and other chief executives, have overall responsibility for how their organizations perform. In coordination with legislators, they establish goals and objectives and then organize programs and form policies to attain these goals. They appoint people to head departments, such as highway, health, police, park and recreation, economic development, and finance. Through these department heads, chief executives oversee the work of civil servants, who carry out programs and enforce laws enacted by the legislative bodies. They prepare budgets, specifying how government resources will be used. They ensure that their government uses resources properly and carries out programs as planned by holding staff conferences, requiring work schedules and periodic performance reports, and conducting personal inspections.

Chief executives meet with legislators and constituents to solicit their ideas, discuss programs, and encourage their support. They also may confer with leaders of other governments to solve mutual problems. Chief executives nominate citizens for government boards and commissions to oversee government activities or examine and help the government solve problems such as drug abuse, crime, deteriorating roads, and inadequate public education.

They also solicit bids from and select contractors to do work for the government, encourage business investment and economic development in their jurisdictions, and seek federal or state funds.

Chief executives of large jurisdictions rely on a staff of aides and assistants, but those in small ones often do much of the work themselves. City, county, town, and other managers, although appointed officials, may act as, and refer to themselves as, chief executives.

Legislators are the elected officials who make laws or amend existing ones in order to remedy problems or to promote certain activities. They include U.S. senators and representatives, state senators and representatives (called assemblymen and assemblywomen, or delegates in some states), county legislators (called supervisors, commissioners, councillors, council members, or freeholders in some states), and city and town council members (called aldermen and alderwomen, trustees, clerks, supervisors, magistrates, and commissioners, among other titles).

Legislators introduce bills to the legislative body and examine and vote on bills introduced by other legislators. In preparing legislation, they read reports and work with constituents, representatives of interest groups, members of boards and commissions, the chief executive and department heads, consultants, and legislators in other units of government. They also approve budgets and the appointments of department heads and commission members submitted by the chief executive. In some jurisdictions, the legislative body appoints a city, town, or county manager. Many legislators, especially at the state and federal levels, have a staff to help do research, prepare legislation, and resolve constituents' problems.

In some units of government, the line between legislative and executive functions blurs. For example, mayors and city managers may draft legislation and conduct council meetings, and council members may oversee the operation of departments.

Government Bigwigs on the Job

Working conditions of chief executives and legislators vary depending on the size of the governmental unit. Time spent at work ranges from meeting once a month for a local council member to sixty or more hours per week for a legislator. U.S. senators and representatives, governors and lieutenant governors, and chief executives and legislators in some large local jurisdictions work full-time year-round, as do almost all county and city managers.

Some city and town managers work for several small jurisdictions. Most state legislators work full-time while legislatures are in session (usually for a few months a year) and part-time the rest of the year. Local elected officials in most jurisdictions work part-time; however, even though the job is officially designated part-time, some incumbents actually work a full-time schedule.

In addition to their regular schedules, chief executives are on call at all hours to handle emergencies.

Some jobs require only occasional out-of-town travel, but others involve more frequent travel, often to attend sessions of the legislature or to meet with officials of other units of government. Officials in districts covering a large area may drive long distances to perform their regular duties.

Employment Figures

About five of six government chief executives and legislators work in local government; the rest work primarily in state governments. The federal government has 535 senators and representatives and two chief executives—the president and vice president. There are about seventy-five hundred state legislators and, according to the International City/County Management Association (ICMA), about eleven thousand city managers.

Chief executives and legislators who do not hold full-time, year-round positions normally work in a second occupation as well (commonly the one they held before being elected), are retired from another occupation, or attend to household responsibilities. Business owner or manager, teacher, and lawyer are common second occupations, and there are many others as well.

Training for Government Bigwigs

Choosing from among candidates who meet the minimum age, residency, and citizenship requirements, the voters try to elect the individual who they decide is most fit to hold the position at stake. Successful candidates usually have a strong record of accomplishment in paid and unpaid work. Many have business, teaching, or legal experience, but others come from a wide variety of occupations. In addition, many have served as volunteers (sometimes as elected members) on school boards or zoning commissions; with charities, political action groups, and political campaigns; or with religious, fraternal, and similar organizations.

Work experience and public service help develop the planning, organizing, negotiating, motivating, fundraising, budgeting, public speaking, and problem-solving skills needed to run a political campaign. Candidates must make decisions quickly and fairly with little or contradictory information. They must have confidence in themselves and their employees to inspire and motivate their constituents and their staff. They should also be sincere and candid, presenting their views thoughtfully and convincingly.

Additionally, they must know how to hammer out compromises with colleagues and constituents. National and statewide campaigns also require a good deal of energy, stamina, and fundraising ability.

Town, city, and county managers are appointed by a council or commission. Managers come from a variety of educational backgrounds. A master's degree in public administration, including courses such as public financial management and legal issues in public administration, is widely recommended but not required. Virtually all town, city, and county managers have at least bachelor's degrees and many hold master's degrees. In addition, working as a student intern in government is recommended. The experience and personal contacts acquired can prove invaluable in eventually securing a position as a town, city, or county manager.

Generally, a town, city, or county manager in a smaller jurisdiction is required to have some expertise in a wide variety of areas; those who work for larger jurisdictions specialize in financial, administrative, or personnel matters. For all managers, communication skills and the ability to get along with others are essential.

Getting Ahead

Advancement opportunities for most elected public officials are not clearly defined. Because elected positions normally require a period of residency and because local public support is critical, officials can usually advance to other offices only in the jurisdictions where they live. For example, council members may run for mayor or for a position in the state government, and state legislators may run for governor or for Congress. Many officials are not politically ambitious, however, and do not seek advancement. Others lose their bids for reelection or voluntarily leave the occupation. A lifetime career as a government chief executive or legislator is rare.

Town, city, and county managers have a clearer career path: obtain a master's degree in public administration, then gain experience as a management analyst or as an assistant in a government department with a council and chief executive and learn about planning, budgeting, civil engineering, and other aspects of running a city. After several years, they may be hired to manage towns or small cities and may eventually become managers of progressively larger cities.

What It's Really Like

Meet Jonas Martin Frost— U.S. Representative

Democrat Jonas Martin Frost was elected to Congress in 1978 as a representative from Texas in the Dallas–Ft. Worth area. He graduated from the University of Missouri in Columbia in 1966 with two degrees—a B.A. and a B.Jour. (journalism). He earned his J.D. degree from Georgetown University, Washington, D.C., in 1972. Prior to coming to Congress he was a reporter for the

Wilmington, Delaware, daily newspaper and the *Congressional Quarterly* in Washington, and then practiced law in Dallas.

He began his service in the U.S. House of Representatives in January of 1979 and has served continuously since that date.

How Congressman Frost Got Started

"During the time of my employment by *Congressional Quarterly*, where I covered the events in Congress, I became convinced that I could be a good representative, serving the interests of my home district in Dallas, Texas. The experience at CQ gave me the insight and contacts within the House of Representatives to achieve a good start once I was elected in 1978.

"My first job was as a staff person on the old Ft. Worth Press, which is no longer in existence. That gave me the experience to move to a daily newspaper and later to join a television panel in Dallas, where I reported on legal matters within the community. The program was called Newsroom, and its anchor was Jim Lehrer during the time he was in Dallas.

"I decided to run for Congress and I knew it was important to pick a district in which I'd feel comfortable . . . with how you think the district feels on issues and with the customs of the area. The Dallas–Ft. Worth area was good for me, as I was born in Ft. Worth, Texas, and was familiar with the Dallas–Ft. Worth area.

"I went about talking to various known community leaders, political activists, and media representatives . . . all of whom would know the political atmosphere of the community. I was running against an incumbent congressman and there is always a group that opposes an incumbent, so it was a bit easier to create a political organization on that basis, rather than running in a district in which no incumbent was running.

"I chose the Democratic party because I believe the general philosophy of the party is closer to my own . . . feelings on how people should be treated by the government, what role the government plays in daily lives, the extent to which government should develop, etc. This is a very personal consideration that comes after years of watching the direction in which a particular party will lead the nation when that party is in power.

"I chose to run for the House rather than the Senate for several reasons. One: I had familiarity with the total area in which I would be running, rather than having to run statewide in Texas . . . that's a large area. Two: I was able to raise enough money to conduct a good campaign on the local level. The cost of running statewide would not have been within my reach at the time of my election to the House. Three: I was familiar with the rules and operations of the House from my days as a reporter for the *Congressional Quarterly*, where I covered the proceedings of the House.

"I lost the first election in 1974. I was very disappointed, but never had the slightest doubt that I would run again. I had received 46 percent of the vote in 1974, so it seemed that the goal was obtainable. After my loss in 1974, I practiced law until winning the election four years later, in 1978.

"There are no term limits for serving in the U.S. House of Representatives. I am currently in my ninth two-year term. (The House has two-year terms. The Senate has six-year terms.)

"I have no plans to leave congressional service. If I were to retire or leave the service of the Congress for any reason, I would likely return to the practice of law in Dallas."

Congressman Frost—on the Job

"My responsibilities now are to vote on issues that are important to my district and the nation as a whole. I represent over 566,000 people in the U.S. Congress, and while it is difficult to represent all of them on the same issues, I must try to bring as many pertinent facts together to make a decision on issues in the best interest of these groups.

"My typical day begins around 6:00 A.M., and generally goes until about 10:00 each evening. The simple things that are associated with the position are the receptions, constituent meetings—where I inform them as to what has happened in Congress—and the other ceremonies that are attached to the position, such as swearing-in ceremonies for new citizens or constituents who are named to positions of trust [public offices], and dedications of new businesses in the district, and so on.

"The difficult part of the day is spending endless hours in committee meetings, where you gain information on bills and resolutions that may affect millions of people in the nation—bills such as mandating young men to register for the draft; determining the amount of income tax that will be taken from all Americans; the Pure Water Act, which protects the drinking water of the nation; the Environmental Protection Act, which dictates how to clean up toxic waste sites in America; international trade legislation, such as NAFTA, which regulates the amount of trade that may be tax free from Mexico and other nations.

"The job can be very tiring, especially the many trips on airplanes that are required to return to my congressional district to make personal appearances to report on the activities of Congress and to meet with constituents about problems they are having—in an effort to help them if I can. There are always a variety of problems: sons or daughters wanting to get into military academies; companies unilaterally trying to eliminate health insurance programs for their retired employees; obtaining emergency loans for farmers who lose crops because of drought or flood—that sort of thing.

"The work atmosphere is enjoyable. The Congress of the United States is generally composed of hardworking men and women who spend many hours in their efforts to make the United States a better nation. Washington, D.C., is our historic capital, and it is always a thrill and honor to be able to work here as I do.

"I like having the opportunity to have direct input into the decision-making function for our government. I represent more than 566,000 people on every issue that I vote on, and few people ever have that chance."

Advice from Congressman Frost

"If you have a desire to serve in public office, you should be absolutely sure of your willingness to serve long hours and to take a lot of criticism for your decisions—because you cannot represent everyone's position on every issue.

"If you make the decision that you want to seek public office . . . then do so. It is a meaningful experience in just seeking the office, whether you win or lose. I lost the first race I made for Congress. Four years later, I still had the dream of serving in the Congress. I ran again, and won."

Bigwigs, Big Bucks?

Earnings of public administrators vary widely, depending on the size of the government unit and on whether the job is full-time and year-round, part-time, or full-time for only a few months a year. Salaries range from little or nothing for a small town council member to $200,000 a year for the president of the United States.

According to the International City/County Management Association (ICMA), the average annual salary of mayors runs about $10,000. In cities with a population under twenty-five hundred, salaries averaged $1,800; in cities with a population over one million, around $78,000.

ICMA data indicate that the average salary for county managers is about $70,000 and $66,000 for city managers. Salaries ranged from $35,000 in towns with fewer than twenty-five hundred residents to $127,000 in cities with a population over one million.

According to *Book of the States, 1994–95*, published by the Council of State Governments, gubernatorial annual salaries ranged from $60,000 in Arkansas to $130,000 in New York. In addition to salary, most governors receive perquisites such as transportation and an official residence. Lieutenant governors average over $57,000 annually.

In 1995, U.S. senators and representatives earned $133,600; the senate and house majority and minority leaders $148,400; and the vice president earned $171,500.

CHAPTER THREE

Education Administrators

S mooth operation of an educational institution requires competent administrators. Education administrators provide direction, leadership, and day-to-day management of educational activities in schools, colleges and universities, businesses, correctional institutions, museums, and job training and community service organizations.

The Role of Education Administrators

Education administrators set educational standards and goals and aid in establishing policies and procedures to carry them out. They develop academic programs; train and motivate teachers and other staff; manage guidance and other student services; administer record keeping; prepare budgets; handle relations with parents, prospective students, employers, or others outside of education; and perform numerous other activities.

They supervise subordinate managers, management support staff, teachers, counselors, librarians, coaches, and others. In an organization such as a small day-care center, there may be one administrator who handles all functions. In a major university or large school system, responsibilities are divided among many administrators, each with a specific function.

Elementary and Secondary School Administrators

Principals

Principals manage elementary and secondary schools. They set the academic tone. High-quality instruction is their main responsibility. Principals assign teachers and other staff, help them improve their skills, and evaluate them. They confer with them—advising, explaining, or answering procedural questions. They visit classrooms, review instructional objectives, and examine learning materials. They also meet with other administrators, students, parents, and representatives of community organizations. They prepare budgets and reports on various subjects, including finances, health, and attendance, and oversee the requisitioning and allocation of supplies. As school budgets become tighter, many principals are trying to encourage financial support for their schools from local businesses.

In recent years, as schools have become more involved with students' emotional welfare as well as academic achievements, schools are providing more services to students. As a result, principals face new responsibilities. For example, in response to the growing number of teenage parents and dual-income single-parent families, more schools have before- and after-school child-care programs or family resource centers, which also may offer parenting classes and social service referrals. With the help of other community organizations, principals also may establish programs to combat the increase in crime, drug and alcohol abuse, and sexually transmitted disease among students.

Assistant Principals

Assistant principals aid the principal in the overall administration of the school. Depending on the number of students, a school may have more than one assistant principal or may not have any. Assistant principals are responsible for scheduling classes and coordinating transportation, custodial, cafeteria, and other support services. They usually handle discipline, social and recreational programs, and health and safety. They also may counsel students on personal, educational, or vocational matters.

Other Administrators

Superintendents oversee entire school districts, interacting with the school board and with principals and administrators at all elementary and secondary schools within the district. They are the top administrators with responsibility for hiring school principals, monitoring overall effectiveness of schools, planning district-wide budgets, and preparing requests for school funding.

Central office administrators manage public schools in school district central offices. This group includes those who direct subject-area programs such as English, music, vocational education, special education, and mathematics. They plan, evaluate, and improve curriculums and teaching techniques and help teachers improve their skills and learn about new methods and materials. They oversee career counseling programs and testing that measures students' abilities and helps place them in appropriate classes.

Central office administrators also include directors of programs such as guidance, school psychology, athletics, curriculum and instruction, and professional development. With the trend toward site-based management, principals and assistant principals, along with teachers and other staff, have primary responsibility for many of these programs in their individual schools.

College and University Administrators

Deans

Academic deans, also known as deans of faculty, provosts, or university deans, assist college or university presidents and develop budgets and academic policies and programs. They direct and coordinate activities of deans of individual colleges and chairpersons of academic departments.

Department Heads

College or university department heads or chairpersons are in charge of departments such as English, biological science, or mathematics. They coordinate schedules of classes and teaching assignments; propose budgets; recruit, interview, and hire applicants for teaching positions; evaluate faculty members; and perform other administrative duties in addition to teaching.

Other Higher Education Administrators

Deans of students (also known as vice presidents of student affairs or student life or directors of student services) direct and coordinate admissions, foreign student services, and health and counseling services, as well as social, recreation, and related programs. In a small college, they may counsel students.

Registrars are custodians of students' education records. They register students, prepare student transcripts, evaluate academic records, oversee the preparation of college catalogs and schedules of classes, and analyze registration statistics.

Directors of admissions manage the process of recruiting and admitting students and work closely with financial aid directors, who oversee scholarship, fellowship, and loan programs. Directors of student activities plan and arrange social, cultural, and recreational activities; assist student-run organizations; and may orient new students. Athletic directors plan and direct intramural and intercollegiate athletic activities, including publicity for athletic events, preparation of budgets, and supervision of coaches.

Education Administrators on the Job

Education administrators hold management positions with significant responsibility. Coordinating and interacting with faculty, parents, and students can be fast-paced and stimulating, but also stressful and demanding. Some jobs include travel.

Principals and assistant principals whose main duty is discipline may find working with difficult students frustrating, but challenging.

Most education administrators work more than forty hours a week, including many nights and weekends when school activities take place. Unlike teachers, they usually work year-round.

Employment Figures

About nine out of ten education administrators work in educational services in elementary, secondary, and technical schools and colleges and universities. The rest worked in child day-care centers, religious organizations, job training centers, state departments of education, and businesses and other organizations that provide training activities for their employees.

Training for Education Administrators

Education administration is not usually an entry-level job. Many education administrators begin their careers in related occupations and prepare for a job in education administration by completing master's or doctoral degrees. Because of the diversity of duties and levels of responsibility, their educational backgrounds and experiences vary considerably.

Principals, assistant principals, central office administrators, and academic deans usually have taught or held other related jobs before moving into administration. Some teachers move directly into principalships; however, most gain experience as an assistant principal or in a central office administrative job.

Getting Ahead

In some cases, administrators move up from related staff jobs such as recruiter, residence hall director, or financial aid or admissions counselor. Earning a higher degree generally improves one's advancement opportunities in education administration.

To be considered for education administrator positions, workers must first prove themselves in their current jobs. In evaluating candidates, supervisors look for determination, confidence, innovativeness, motivation, and managerial attributes, such as ability to make sound decisions and to organize and coordinate work efficiently. Since much of the job involves interacting with others, from students to parents to teachers, administrators must have strong interpersonal skills and be effective communicators and motivators. Knowledge of management principles and practices, gained through work experience and formal education, is important.

Public school principals, assistant principals, and school administrators in central offices generally need a state teaching certificate and a master's degree in education administration or educational supervision. Some principals and central office administrators have doctorates in education administration.

In private schools, administrators often have master's or doctoral degrees, but may hold only bachelor's degrees, since private schools are not subject to state certification requirements.

Academic deans usually hold doctorates in their subject areas. Admissions, student affairs, and financial aid directors and registrars often start in related staff jobs. Bachelor's degrees in any field usually are acceptable, followed by advanced degrees in college student affairs or higher education administration. Doctorate are usually necessary for top student affairs positions.

Computer literacy and a background in mathematics or statistics may be assets in admissions, records, and financial work.

Advanced degrees in higher education administration, educational supervision, and college student affairs are offered in many colleges and universities. The National Council for Accreditation of Teacher Education accredits programs. Education administration degree programs include courses in school management, school law, school finance and budgeting, curriculum development and evaluation, research design and data analysis, community relations, politics in education, counseling, and leadership. Educational supervision degree programs include courses in supervision of instruction and curriculum, human relations, curriculum development, research, and advanced pedagogy.

Education administrators advance by moving up an administrative ladder or transferring to larger schools or systems. They also may become superintendents of school system or presidents of educational institutions.

The Road Ahead

Substantial competition is expected for prestigious jobs as education administrators. Many teachers and other staff meet the education and experience requirements for these jobs and seek promotion. However, the number of openings is relatively small, so generally only the most highly qualified are selected. Candidates who have the most formal education and who are willing to relocate should have the best job prospects.

Employment of education administrators is expected to grow about as fast as the average for all occupations through the year 2005. Most job openings, particularly for principals and assistant principals, are likely to result from the need to replace administrators who retire. Additional openings will be created by workers who transfer to other occupations.

Employment of education administrators will grow as school enrollments increase; as more services are provided to students; as efforts to improve the quality of education continue; and as institutions comply with government regulations, such as those regarding financial aid.

The number of education administrators employed depends largely on state and local expenditures for education. Budgetary constraints could result in fewer administrators than anticipated; pressures to increase spending to improve the quality of education could result in more.

What It's Really Like

Meet Laura Murray— School Superintendent

Laura Murray is school superintendent with Homewood Flossmoor Community High School District 233 in Flossmoor, Illinois. Her school district won the U.S. Department of Education Blue Ribbon Award for Educational Excellence and a national technology award. Her office is located in one of the district's school buildings.

She earned her bachelor's degree in mathematics from Purdue University in West Lafayette, Indiana, in 1972; her master's in secondary education in 1976 from Northern Illinois University in DeKalb; and her doctorate in 1989 in educational leadership and policy studies from Loyola University in Chicago. She also has a guidance and counseling certificate and has attended numerous professional conferences. She's been working in the education field since 1972.

How Laura Murray Got Started

"I graduated from high school in 1968. Because I'd had such outstanding mathematics teachers, one in particular—Mr. Brown—I decided to major in math. When I graduated from college, the district was building a fourth high school, Glenbard South. The superintendent lived a block from my parents, so I got an interview in a van (because it was on a Sunday and the building was locked). Anyway, I got the job as a full-time high school math teacher.

"The district shifted teachers among the four high schools and Mr. Brown was assigned to Glenbard South, so I got to teach with him, which was an honor. On the first day of teaching they asked us all what we wanted to do in twenty years. I said, 'Be a high school principal.' That occurred nineteen years later. In between, here is what happened:

"After I taught for several years, coached tennis, coached Pom Poms and sponsored Student Council, the principal came to me and said, 'A guidance counselor is pregnant. Get your certificate and the job is yours.' I did. For two years I was a guidance counselor.

"In May of 1980 I had a son. I quit to stay home with him. In July 1980, I was going crazy as I had always worked and I was bored. So I called my old principal and asked if there were any jobs I could have. He said the dean of students was open and that it was all discipline—did I want it? I agreed and did it for two years. During that time I got knocked in the jaw, skunked by a skunk, and had to pick up 1,981 mice that the seniors let go in the cafeteria as a graduation prank.

"In June of 1982 I was called by an area superintendent and asked to be director of guidance at another high school in a different district. I went because I was tired of doing discipline and the new job seemed a challenge. I revamped an entire department and learned that Machiavelli is right. As a leader, you have to learn to be respected—but maybe not liked or loved. That is a hard pill to swallow if you are a people person. After three years in the job and a successful reorganization, I was called by my previous district and asked to come back as assistant principal. My current district did not want to lose me, so they made me the same offer.

"At that time I realized that, to be a high school principal, I would need a Ph.D., so I worked full-time on it while still being a mother, wife, and full-time assistant principal. When it was time to apply to be a principal, I realized it would be the first job I sought since applying as a math teacher. All the others had been offered to me.

"I applied at Homewood Flossmoor High school and got the job. The superintendent, principal, and business manager were all retiring within a three-year span. I had one year as principal to work with the superintendent who had been there for twenty-five years. I loved it. Then a new superintendent was hired. Unfortunately, he lasted only a year and a few months with the Board of Education. The fit wasn't there, so on October 19, 1993, I was named acting superintendent and principal.

"I did both jobs for several months and then the board asked me if I wanted to be superintendent. I had to really think about that because all I ever wanted to be was principal. After much soul-searching and networking with many friends, I decided to say yes. The key here is that I was going from a building-level position to a district position and didn't have any district experience. I was a first, but I am a quick study.

"Part of it was being in the right place at the right time. In Illinois there are only three superintendents of high school districts who are female. I was the second one.

"I entered education because I like students and I believe in public education. I am a real people-oriented person. I had role models in high school whom I really admired, so I chose this profession. The different jobs I had all came about because someone above me thought I would be good at the job and convinced me to try it."

Laura Murray—on the Job

"Officially, the superintendent of schools serves as the chief school officer of the Board of Education. I am responsible for the overall administration and supervision of the educational system and for all personnel and factors that directly or indirectly serve to direct and control the system.

"My key functions include maintaining a relationship with the Board of Education, Instruction, and Curriculum; managing personnel (recommending, hiring, and evaluating); and handling fiscal affairs, management and operations, and community relations.

"The job is very busy and you have to be able to juggle twenty things at once. It is very stressful and requires long hours. Days of twelve and fourteen hours are very typical with many evening and weekend responsibilities.

"I spend much time on the telephone, meeting with people, and being a public relations person. I have learned to be an expert in conflict management and have spoken at many conferences on this topic.

"There is no set schedule. A typical day could include numerous telephone conversations, several meetings with teachers, conferences with students and/or parents, a Rotary meeting, classroom visitations, and meetings with community leaders.

"Also, there could be a crisis, such as a student fight involving a weapon, or there could be an exciting event. We were recently notified that in four days President Clinton would visit our school—that was really fun.

"I love working with students and watching them grow and develop in four years of high school. It is gratifying to be in a position to effect change that will increase student learning, student self-esteem, and student motivation. I like the way no day is typical. I can be proactive, but I have learned how to be reactive in a positive way. I love to be busy and to do several activities at once. I like challenges, and this job is always a challenge or offers a puzzle to solve.

"What I like least is the stress, and sometimes dealing with negative people can be depressing. Also, one of the most important jobs of a superintendent is working with Board of Education members. I have a great board with whom I work, but I imagine it would be quite difficult and no fun working with board members who constantly disagreed with you and among themselves."

Advice from Laura Murray

"First, do as many different jobs in the education setting as you can so you can see things from many viewpoints. Second, learn how to make decisions, deal with conflict, and plan strategically. Third, have outlets in your life that release stress, and learn how to make time for yourself.

"This job also takes a very supportive family who likes to attend high school events."

Earnings for Education Administrators

Salaries of education administrators vary according to position, level of responsibility and experience, and the size and location of the institution. According to the Educational Research Service, average salaries for principals and assistant principals in the school year 1994–95 were as follows:

Principals:

Elementary school	$58,600
Junior high/middle school	$62,300
Senior high school	$66,600

Assistant Principals:

Elementary school	$48,500
Junior high/middle school	$52,900
Senior high school	$55,600

In 1994–95, according to the College and University Personnel Association, median annual salaries for selected administrators in higher education were as follows:

Academic Deans:

Arts and sciences	$79,200
Business	$78,600
Education	$77,700
Engineering	$100,900
Law	$139,000
Mathematics	$56,900
Medicine	$199,500
Social sciences	$58,600

Student Services Directors:

Admissions and registrar	$50,600
Student activities	$33,400
Student financial aid	$43,400

CHAPTER FOUR

Financial Managers

Practically every firm, whether in manufacturing, communications, finance, education, or health care, has one or more financial managers. Some of them are treasurers, controllers, credit managers, cash managers; they prepare the financial reports required by the firm to conduct its operations and to ensure that the firm satisfies tax and regulatory requirements.

Financial managers also oversee the flow of cash and financial instruments, monitor the extension of credit, assess the risk of transactions, raise capital, analyze investments, develop information to assess the present and future financial status of the firm, and communicate with stockholders and other investors.

In small firms, chief financial officers usually handle all financial management functions. However, in large firms, these officers oversee all financial management departments and help top managers develop financial and economic policy and establish procedures, delegate authority, and oversee the implementation of these policies. Highly trained and experienced financial managers head each financial department.

Options in Financial Management

Controllers direct the preparation of all financial reports, such as income statements, balance sheets, and depreciation schedules. They oversee the accounting, audit, or budget departments.

Cash and credit managers monitor and control the flow of cash receipts and disbursements to meet the business and investment needs of the firm. For example, cash flow projections are needed to determine whether loans must be obtained to meet cash requirements, or whether surplus cash may be invested in interest-bearing instruments.

Risk and insurance managers oversee programs to minimize risks and losses that may arise from financial transactions and business operations undertaken by their institutions. Credit operations managers establish credit rating criteria, determine credit ceilings, and monitor their institutions' extension of credit. Reserve officers review their institutions' financial statements and direct the purchase and sale of bonds and other securities to maintain the asset–liability ratio required by law. User representatives in international accounting develop integrated international financial and accounting systems for the banking transactions of multinational organizations.

Financial institutions such as banks, savings and loan associations, credit unions, personal credit institutions, and finance companies may serve as depositories for cash and financial instruments and offer loans, investment counseling, consumer credit, trust management, and other financial services. Some specialize in specific financial services.

Financial managers in financial institutions include, for example, vice presidents, who may head one or more financial departments; bank branch managers; savings and loan association managers; consumer credit managers; and credit union managers. These managers make decisions in accordance with policy set by the institution's board of directors and federal and state laws and regulations.

Due to changing regulations and increased government scrutiny, financial managers in financial institutions must place greater emphasis on accurate reporting of financial data. They must have detailed understanding of industries allied to banking, such as insurance, real estate, and securities, and broad knowledge of business and industrial activities. With growing domestic and foreign competition, knowledge of an expanding and increasingly complex variety of financial services is becoming a necessity for financial managers in financial institutions and other corporations. For international financial institutions, a working knowledge of the financial systems of foreign countries is essential.

Besides supervising financial services, managers in financial institutions may advise individuals and businesses on financial planning.

Financial Managers on the Job

Financial managers are provided with comfortable offices, often close to top managers and to departments that develop the financial data these managers need. Although overtime may sometimes be required, financial managers typically work a forty-hour week. Attendance at meetings of financial and economic associations and similar activities is often required. In very large corporations, some traveling to subsidiary firms and to customer accounts may be necessary.

Employment Figures

Financial managers held about 768,000 jobs in 1994. Although these managers are found in virtually every industry, one-third were employed by financial institutions, banks, savings institutions, finance companies, credit unions, insurance companies, securities dealers, and real estate firms. Nearly another third were employed by services industries, including business, health, social, and management services.

Training for Financial Managers

A bachelor's degree in accounting or finance, or in business administration with an emphasis on accounting or finance, is suitable academic preparation for financial managers. A Master of Business Administration (M.B.A.) degree is increasingly valued by employers. Many financial management positions are filled by promoting experienced, technically skilled professional personnel serving as accountants, budget analysts, credit analysts, insurance analysts, loan officers, securities analysts, and accounting or related department supervisors in large institutions.

Due to the growing complexity of global trade, shifting federal and state laws and regulations, and a proliferation of new, complex financial instruments, continuing education is becoming vital for financial managers. Firms often provide opportunities for workers to broaden their knowledge and skills and encourage employees to take graduate courses at colleges and universities or attend conferences sponsored by the company.

In addition, financial management, banking, and credit union associations, often in cooperation with colleges and universities, sponsor numerous national or local training programs. Attendees prepare extensively at home, then attend sessions on subjects such as accounting management, budget management, corporate cash management, financial analysis, international banking, and data processing and management information systems.

Many firms pay all or part of the costs for those who successfully complete courses. Although experience, ability, and leadership are emphasized for promotion, advancement may be accelerated by this type of special study.

In some cases, financial managers may also broaden their skills and exhibit their competency in specialized fields by attaining professional certification. For example, the Association for Investment Management and Research confers the Chartered Financial Analyst designation to investment professionals who have bachelor's degrees, pass three test levels, and have three or more years of experience in the field.

The National Association of Credit Management administers a three-part certification program for business credit professionals. Through a combination of experience and examinations, these financial managers pass through the level of Credit Business Associate to Credit Business Fellow and then to Certified Credit Executive. The Treasury Management Association confers the Certified Cash Manager designation to those who pass an examination and have two years of relevant experience.

The Qualities You'll Need

Persons interested in becoming financial managers should like to work independently, deal with people, and analyze detailed account information. The ability to communicate, both orally and in writing, is increasingly important. Financial managers also need tact, good judgment, and the ability to establish effective personal relationships to oversee supervisory and professional staff members.

Getting Ahead

Financial analysis and management have been revolutionized by technological improvements in personal computers and data processing equipment. Knowledge of their applications is vital to upgrade managerial skills and to enhance advancement opportunities.

Because financial management is critical for efficient business operations, well-trained, experienced financial managers who display a strong grasp of the operations of various departments within their organization are prime candidates for promotion to top management positions.

Some financial managers transfer to closely related positions in other industries. Those with extensive experience and access to sufficient capital may head their own consulting firms.

Looking Ahead

Like other managerial occupations, the number of applicants for financial management positions is expected to exceed the number of job openings, resulting in competition for jobs. Employment of financial managers is expected to increase about as fast as the average for all occupations through the year 2005.

In addition, job openings will arise each year as financial managers transfer to other occupations, start their own businesses, or retire. Like other managers, most financial managers who leave their jobs seek other positions in their field; relatively few experienced workers leave the occupation permanently each year.

Although the need for skilled financial management will increase due to the demands of global trade, the proliferation of complex financial instruments, and continually changing federal and state laws and regulations, employment growth among financial managers will be tempered by corporate restructuring and downsizing in many industries. Many firms are reducing their ranks of middle managers in an effort to be more efficient and competitive. Similarly, as the banking industry consolidates and banks merge their operations, some financial management positions may be eliminated. These forces will prevent the growing need for skilled financial managers from resulting in dramatic employment growth.

Many opportunities will still exist for the most skilled, adaptable, and knowledgeable financial managers. Those who keep abreast of the latest financial instruments and changing regulations, and those familiar with data processing and management information systems and the range of financial services—such as banking, business credit, credit unions, insurance, real estate, and securities—will enjoy the best employment opportunities. Developing expertise in a rapidly growing industry, such as health care, also may prove helpful.

What It's Really Like

Meet Larry Morin—Senior Vice President, Customer Relations

Larry Morin works as the head of Customer Relations for Fidelity Investments, National Financial Security Corporation, in New York City. He started in the financial field in 1971 and has ten years of regional banking experience in Connecticut and Minnesota and fifteen years in brokerage with Merrill Lynch, Shearson Lehman, and Fidelity Investments.

How Larry Morin Got Started

"It was serendipity. Most people I know did not set out to get the job they have on Wall Street. My neighbor was the head teller of Connecticut Bank and Trust. I needed a part-time job and the bank was starting a new department called *clearance*.

"For every buy or sell of stocks and bonds, there is a corresponding delivery from the seller to the buyer. Each brokerage firm has an operating area that supports the settlement, or clearance, of these transactions. There are bookkeeping entries that reflect the transaction on each customer account. Say you buy a hundred shares of IBM. You buy them from your stock broker. Your broker, in turn, buys them from a broker for IBM. There are actual pieces of paper that cross hands from IBM to your brokerage company. They are 'delivered' and 'cleared' into your account. You also get copies. This is *clearance*. Stocks and bonds, in this case, are called *securities*.

"I took the job and for the next five years, moving to full-time, learned all the functions of this department. My first job there was to walk around to the different banks and deliver securities. When I learned the language and the system, I got hooked. And in many ways, it is just like learning a whole new language. There are a host of settlement and clearance activities for various products that customers transact with brokerage firms, such as government securities, or government bonds, and national securities, or bonds between nations.

"There are also operations that the brokerage firms provide. *Operations* is the name for the departments that take care of any transaction of stocks and bonds, i.e., securities. These operations support activities that occur on securities held in a customer's account—such as dividends, interest, and mergers. These are just a few of what is known in brokerage as 'custody activities,' the way the customer gets custody of the stock or bond. There is special language and knowledge that surround these custody activities.

"I learned that language quickly and looked for shortcuts and precision. I always asked what I could do and if anyone needed help.

"The head teller moved to Investors Diversified Service (IDS) in Minnesota, a major mutual fund and investor advisory firm that is currently owned by American Express. I went with him to set up another clearance department. From there, I was introduced by a friend of his to Merrill Lynch. I did the same as far as learning the language and the system. I was still hooked. I wrote an instructional book that saved them time and money.

"While moving up the corporate ladder from manager to senior vice president, I learned many aspects of the brokerage field. In Merrill, I learned operations. In Shearson, I ran operations and 'the cage,' which is the vault. Now, I'm running customer service."

Larry Morin—on the Job

"Now I manage an organization of between one hundred and five hundred people, with five to eight people who report directly to me. I generally spend time overseeing the day-to-day functions: customer service, tax reporting, transfer of accounts between firms, retirement account processing, opening new accounts, gain and loss reporting, and mail operations.

"I also look at management reports and seek new ways of improving processing and service. In meetings with the people who report directly to me, I challenge them on numbers, trends, and performance, targeting improvement opportunities and trying to initiate people's thinking about the day-to-day and 'what ifs' (out-of-box thinking). I do this by asking questions about how to improve processing, by reducing rejects or things that have to be reprocessed because of mistakes. I initiate questions in our staff meetings that help the staff look at a problem in new ways in order to solve it. One of these ways is through brainstorming, where everyone throws out suggestions and we build from everyone's input.

"Each day is different, depending on the status of meeting and reports. Sometimes, I may walk into work and have to spend a morning dealing with a problem, even though I was supposed to be at another appointed meeting. My work week is between forty-five and fifty hours, and I work in a friendly, interactive environment.

"When you arrive at a breakthrough idea and see it implemented is the upside to this job. People then embrace the vision (the project) and grow with it.

"My management style is that of empowering people to manage their own organizations and take risks and be self-starters. I also like to interact with employees on all levels. As such, I am able to get a grassroots understanding of all employee contributions. I support and sponsor employee recognition, incentives, 'employee of the month,' special bonuses, merit awards, and letters of commendation. I also single out employees for special training. Outside of this, I believe in verbal praise. The company backs my support. I enjoy rewarding people through recognition and having them appreciate it and seeing trusting relationships develop.

"It's great to be a part of a growing and intellectually stimulating environment and to flourish in this environment, plus interacting with all staff at all levels. But, like any corporation, there is a lot of unnecessary bureaucratic red tape. I don't like when there's a lot of politics around people's vested interests that do not have to do with the process of the project or department. We all have vested interests, but the guidelines of the department as well as the interest of the customers must come first. Some people have a vested interest in making themselves look good. They do not hire people who will challenge them, so their job is always safe. They do not give credit to people under them, giving it to themselves instead.

"Another downside is that there have been times in my career when bosses a level or two above would not let me manage. They would tell me what to do and expect me to be a robot and carry out their orders in their style. Often they were dictatorial. They would not empower me. They would not say 'I want this done . . . just do it' and let me use my style and trust it would get done.

"Good leaders empower their people. They ask them to do things, let them go and do it their way, and ask for a report about how it is going. You need to have some boundaries and reports and weekly update meetings. These are a ways of making sure it is getting done."

Advice from Larry Morin

"One: Learn the language and the system.

"Two: Understand what is important to you and what your values are. You'll be tested around business ethics and management. When you manage one hundred to five hundred people, this issue comes up often. People always push for the bottom line—do more, sell more, reduce expenses. There will be times in your career that you face decisions that are not black and white, but more gray. For example: you have to reduce staff and it comes down to two employees, both rated the same. One employee started the day before the other employee. The newer employee happens to be a friend of the manager. That manager comes to you and suggests that you save that person's job, saying to you, 'After all, it's only a day.' To top it off, you are friends with the manager. What do you do? This situation will test your values and your business ethics.

"Three: Make it a game and don't get too attached. Let the process develop—give logic a chance to prevail. Learn the environment and don't force fit your idea. Remember that not all decisions have to be made immediately. Live with any decision awhile. Give yourself 'time-outs' to reflect so you don't get too caught up.

"Four: Be open to luck and go with it.

"Five: Be open to relationship development, either from a potential mentor or a future student. People tend to create allegiances and teams, then mentor an individual, as the head teller did for me. It's a give-and-take relationship. First you give, they take, and then they give. If they advance, you advance. Everyone wants to attach to the people on the move who can create a learning environment.

"Six: Look to the next position you want—how it will promote you and what you want from your career."

Meet Diane Camerlo—In-House Counsel, Federal Reserve Bank

Diane Camerlo works with four other lawyers in the legal department of the Federal Reserve Bank of St. Louis. She received her B.A. from Denison University in Granville, Ohio. In 1976, she earned her J.D. from Franklin Pierce Law Center in Concord, New Hampshire. She has been practicing law for more than twenty years.

How Diane Camerlo Got Started

"When I graduated from college with a B.A. in sociology and English, I realized my career choices were limited to low-level jobs that would only lead to careers that didn't interest me. I considered various graduate school options and chose law because I believed lawyers did interesting, challenging work and were well paid and highly respected. My father had practiced law before taking a business position, so the field was familiar to me.

"In 1976 I began working as an associate in a law firm in Toledo, Ohio, and then later became a partner. The firm had about thirty-five to forty-five lawyers. I practiced mostly antitrust law, including complex litigation, but when Reagan dried up antitrust I did workers' comp. That was frustrating after antitrust, so later I quit and moved to Rochester, New York, and sold computers until my daughter was born. I then took a law/business/computer job with a former legal client, a bank, and then I took a job in the Monsanto corporate legal department doing antitrust and general corporate work. I was only a contractor in that job (i.e., no benefits), so when the Fed job opened, I took it. Thus, I've had experience in just about every way a lawyer can have experience except as a prosecutor, public defender, or judge."

Diane Camerlo—on the Job

"The Federal Reserve Bank of St. Louis is one of the twelve operating arms of the Federal Reserve System located throughout the nation that, together with their twenty-five branches, carry out various system functions, including operating a nationwide payments system, distributing the nation's currency and coin, supervising and regulating member banks and bank holding companies, and serving as banker for the U.S. Treasury.

"My day is usually made up of some combination of meetings, client counseling, research, writing, planning, public speaking, telephone calls, traveling, and administrative duties. I could spend an entire day doing any one of those things, or I could do all of those things during the course of the day. I also attend continuing legal education seminars from time to time and serve on business-related committees and task forces.

"In my law department the lawyers don't have rigidly defined areas of specialization, so each of us works on a wide variety of projects. The areas of law might include: employment, employee benefits, contract, commercial, intellectual property, banking, general corporate, antitrust, environmental, safety, technology, tax, litigation, or just about anything else. Most of my work involves contract, employment, banking, or technology law. I also review bank holding-company applications required to be filed with the Federal Reserve. And we monitor pending federal and state legislation that affects our industry.

"I am usually very busy with twenty or more active projects going on at one time. During the week I work nine to ten hours on a typical day, though I sometimes work a much longer (or occasionally shorter) day.

"The atmosphere in my law department is businesslike and friendly. The lawyers usually work on individual projects, but we frequently confer with each other. This give and take among attorneys enables us to provide better legal advice to our clients and also makes the job more rewarding.

"I like the intellectual challenge and stimulation of practicing law. I like working in a corporation where I can understand the business in depth and work with the businesspeople to achieve the corporation's goals. I also enjoy the supportive atmosphere in our legal department.

"The primary downside to practicing law is the high level of pressure. Lawyers must give accurate legal advice, often with very short time limits. Another downside is the confrontational nature of the legal practice. Fortunately, this is much less a factor in an in-house corporate practice than in a law firm practice. Finally, the low opinion of lawyers held by the general public is sometimes hard to take. While there are some bad apples in the legal profession, as in all professions, in my law department we place a high value on ethical behavior and client service."

Advice from Diane Camerlo

"For anyone considering a career in law I would recommend going to the best law school possible and getting the highest grades possible. Grades are especially important. The market for new lawyers is tight, and those with low grades will have more trouble getting a job than those with high grades."

Salaries for Financial Managers

The median annual salary of financial managers was $39,700 in 1994. The lowest 10 percent earned $20,200 or less, while the top 10 percent earned over $77,800.

According to a 1995 survey by Robert Half International, a staffing services firm specializing in accounting and finance, salaries of chief financial officers/treasurers ranged from $60,000 in the smallest firms to $295,000 in the largest firms;

controllers, $46,000 to $134,000; and assistant controllers, $40,000 to $77,800.

The salary level depends upon the manager's experience and the size and location of the organization and is likely to be higher in large organizations and cities. Many financial managers in private industry receive additional compensation in the form of bonuses, which also vary substantially by size of firm.

CHAPTER FIVE

Marketing and Sales Managers

A s we learned in Chapter 1, managers work in almost any corporate setting and play many different roles. In this chapter we'll have a close-up look at marketing, sales, advertising, promotion, and public relations managers.

The fundamental objective of any firm is to market its products or services profitably. In small firms, all marketing responsibilities may be assumed by the owner or chief executive officer. In large firms, which may offer numerous products and services nationally or even worldwide, experienced marketing, advertising, and public relations managers coordinate these and related activities.

Marketing Managers

The executive vice president for marketing in a large firm directs the overall marketing policy, including market research, marketing strategy, sales, advertising, promotion, pricing, product development, and public relations activities. These activities are supervised by middle and supervisory managers who oversee staffs of professionals and technicians.

Marketing managers develop the firm's detailed marketing strategy. With the help of subordinates, including product development managers and market research managers, they determine the demand for products and services offered by the firm and its competitors and identify potential consumers such as business firms, wholesalers, retailers, government, or the general public. Mass markets are further categorized according to factors such as region, age, income, and lifestyle.

Marketing managers develop pricing strategy with an eye toward maximizing the firm's share of the market and its profits while ensuring that the firm's customers are satisfied. In collaboration with sales, product development, and other managers, they monitor trends that indicate the need for new products and services and oversee product development.

Marketing managers work with advertising and promotion managers to best promote the firm's products and services and to attract potential users.

Sales Managers

Sales managers direct the firm's sales program. They assign sales territories and goals and establish training programs for their sales representatives. Managers advise their sales representatives on ways to improve their sales performance. In large, multiproduct firms, they oversee regional and local sales managers and their staffs. Sales managers maintain contact with dealers and distributors. They analyze sales statistics gathered by their staffs and monitor the preferences of customers to determine sales potential and inventory requirements. Such information is vital to develop products and maximize profits.

Advertising Managers

Except in the largest firms, advertising and promotion staffs are generally small and serve as a liaison between the firm and the advertising or promotion agency to which many advertising or promotional functions are contracted out.

Advertising managers oversee the account services, creative services, and media services departments. The account services department is managed by account executives, who assess the need for advertising and, in advertising agencies, maintain the accounts of clients.

The creative services department develops the subject matter and presentation of advertising. This department is supervised by a creative director, who oversees the copy chief and art director and their staffs. The media services department is supervised by the media director, who oversees planning groups that select the communication media—radio, television, newspapers, magazines, or outdoor signs—to disseminate the advertising.

Promotion Managers

Promotion managers supervise staffs of promotion specialists. They direct promotion programs combining advertising with purchase incentives to increase sales of products or services. In an effort to establish closer contact with purchasers, dealers, distributors, or consumers, promotion programs may involve direct mail, telemarketing, television or radio advertising, catalogs, exhibits, newspaper inserts, in-store displays, product endorsements, or special events. Purchase incentives may include discounts, samples, gifts, rebates, coupons, sweepstakes, or contests.

Public Relations Managers

Public relations managers supervise public relations specialists. These managers direct publicity programs to a targeted public. They use any necessary communication media in their effort to maintain the support of the specific group upon whom their organization's success depends, such as consumers, stockholders, or the general public. For example, public relations managers may clarify or justify the firm's point of view on health or environmental issues to community or special-interest groups. They may evaluate advertising and promotion programs for compatibility with public relations efforts.

Public relations managers, in effect, serve as the eyes and ears of top management. They observe social, economic, and political trends that might ultimately have an effect upon the firm. They make recommendations to enhance the firm's public image in view of those trends. Public relations managers may confer with labor relations managers to produce internal company communications, such as news about employee–management relations, and with financial managers to produce company reports. They may assist company executives in drafting speeches or arranging interviews and other forms of public contact; oversee company archives; and respond to information requests. In addition, public relations managers may handle special events such as sponsorship of races, parties introducing new products, or other activities the firm supports in order to gain public attention through the press without advertising directly.

Managers on the Job

Marketing, advertising, and public relations managers are provided with offices close to the top managers. Long hours, including evenings and weekends, are common. Working under pressure is unavoidable as schedules change, problems arise, and deadlines and goals must be met.

Marketing, advertising, and public relations managers meet frequently with other managers. Some meet with the public and with government officials.

Substantial travel may be involved. For example, attendance at meetings sponsored by associations or industries is often mandatory. Sales managers travel to national, regional, and local offices and to various dealers and distributors. Advertising and promotion managers may travel to meet with clients or representatives of communication media. Public relations managers may travel to meet with special-interest groups or government officials. Job transfers between headquarters and regional offices are common, particularly among sales managers, and may disrupt family life.

Marketing, advertising, and public relations managers are found in virtually every industry. Industries employing them in significant numbers include motor vehicle dealers, printing and publishing firms, advertising agencies, department stores, computer and data processing services firms, and management and public relations firms.

Training for Managers

Many educational backgrounds are suitable for entry into marketing, advertising, and public relations managerial jobs, but many employers prefer a broad liberal arts background. Bachelor's degrees in sociology, psychology, literature, or philosophy, among other subjects, are acceptable. However, requirements vary depending upon the particular job.

For marketing, sales, and promotion management positions, some employers prefer bachelor's or master's degrees in business administration with emphasis on marketing. Courses in business law, economics, accounting, finance, mathematics, and statistics are also highly recommended.

In highly technical industries, such as computer and electronics manufacturing, bachelor's degrees in engineering or science combined with master's degrees in business administration may be preferred. (See Chapter 6 to learn about careers in engineering management.)

For advertising management positions, some employers prefer bachelor's degrees in advertising or journalism. A course of study should include marketing, consumer behavior, market research, sales, communications methods and technology, and visual arts courses such as art history and photography.

For public relations management positions, some employers prefer bachelor's or master's degrees in public relations or journalism. The curriculum should include courses in advertising, business administration, public affairs, political science, and creative and technical writing. For all these specialties, management courses and internships are highly recommended. Familiarity with computerized word processing and database applications also are important for many marketing, advertising, and public relations management positions.

Most marketing, advertising, and public relations management positions are filled by promoting experienced staff or related professional or technical personnel such as sales representatives, purchasing agents, buyers, product or brand specialists, advertising specialists, promotion specialists, and public relations specialists.

In small firms, where the number of positions is limited, advancement to a management position may come slowly. In large firms, promotion may occur more quickly.

Although experience, ability, and leadership are emphasized for promotion, advancement may be accelerated by participation in management training programs conducted by many large firms. Many firms also provide their employees with continuing education opportunities—either in-house or at local colleges and universities—and encourage employee participation in seminars and conferences, usually provided by professional societies. Often in collaboration with colleges and universities, numerous marketing and related associations sponsor national or local management training programs. Courses include brand and product management, international marketing, sales management evaluation, telemarketing and direct sales, promotion, marketing communication, market research, organizational communication, and data processing systems procedures and management. Many firms pay all or part of the cost for those who successfully complete courses.

Some associations (listed in the Appendix) offer certification programs for marketing, advertising, and public relations managers. Certification is a sign of competence and achievement, which is particularly important in a competitive job market. While relatively few marketing, advertising, and public relations managers currently are certified, the number of managers who seek certification is expected to grow. For example, Sales and Marketing Executives International offers a management certification program based on education and job performance. The Public Relations Society of America offers an accreditation program for public relations practitioners based on years of experience and an examination. The American Marketing Association is developing a certification program for marketing managers.

Those interested in becoming marketing, advertising, and public relations managers should be mature, creative, highly motivated, resistant to stress, and flexible, yet decisive. The ability to communicate persuasively, both orally and in writing, with other managers, staff, and the public is vital.

Marketing, advertising, and public relations managers also need tact, good judgment, and exceptional ability to establish and maintain effective personal relationships with supervisory and professional staff members and client firms.

Getting Ahead

Because of the importance and high visibility of their jobs, marketing, advertising, and public relations managers often are prime candidates for advancement. Well-trained, experienced, successful managers may be promoted to higher positions in their own or other firms. Some become top executives. Managers with extensive experience and sufficient capital may open their own businesses.

The Road Ahead

Employment of marketing, advertising, and public relations managers is expected to increase faster than the average for all occupations through the year 2005. Increasingly intense domestic and global competition in products and services offered to consumers should require greater marketing, promotional, and public relations efforts.

Projected employment growth varies by industry. Management and public relations firms may experience particularly rapid growth as businesses increasingly hire contractors for these services rather than support additional full-time staff. Employment of marketing, advertising, and public relations managers is expected to grow much faster than average in most business services industries, such as computer and data processing, while average growth is projected in manufacturing industries overall.

In addition to faster-than-average growth, many job openings will occur each year as a result of managers moving into top management positions, transferring to other jobs, or leaving the labor force. However, other managers or highly experienced professional and technical personnel will be seeking these highly coveted jobs, resulting in substantial job competition. College graduates with extensive experience, a high level of creativity, and strong communication skills should have the best job opportunities.

What It's Really Like

Meet Chris Fuller—General Manager, Marketing and Sales, Food Services

Chris Fuller worked his way up in the food services industry through a variety of responsible positions. He worked at Colgate Palmolive, Pepsi Cola, and Thomas J. Lipton and retired in 1988.

How Chris Fuller Got Started

"What attracted me to this field was that it was kind of glamorous. You had a lot of advertising and promotion. Product managers made good money, the businesses were stable, and you didn't have the big hiring and firing problems we have in the nineties. You could stay with a company for a long time. They had good programs and they were well respected in the business community all around the United States.

"I got my B.A. in economics and my M.B.A., both at Dartmouth College. That was back in 1953. I've been in this business for thirty years. I started with Colgate Palmolive in 1956. It wasn't a food business, but analogous to it; it was in the household products business, which sold products through the same channels as the food companies. The products ended up in the same stores.

"At General Foods I was manager of marketing analysis and then became a product manager in the frozen potato business. At Pepsi Cola I was vice president of finance and president of Metrop Bottling Company, which sold Pepsi through company-owned franchises in the United States.

"I went to work for Thomas J. Lipton in 1977 and had never been in food service before. I was senior vice president of operations and finance there, then became senior vice president of general management. That was a marketing job, where I managed a group of businesses including the food service end."

Chris Fuller—on the Job

"Food service is a secondary business within the framework of a retail business in most food companies—General Foods, or Nabisco, or Proctor and Gamble, for example. Food service is usually a much smaller part of their business and normally a less profitable part of the business.

"The purpose of the food service industry, at least at Thomas J. Lipton, was to sell company products, such as tea bags, and get them exposed in restaurants and cafeterias—wherever food was sold throughout the United States. The retail end deals with supermarkets and smaller mom-and-pop stores.

"There are several functions in a food service business. One is to take the products that a retail business is selling and get them designed in the right sizes and the right types of packages to sell to restaurants. You don't necessarily sell the same product to a restaurant that you would to a consumer through a food store.

"You have to take the entire line of products you want to sell to restaurants and have them redesigned for the restaurant trade. When I was there, the major product happened to be tea bags. A tea bag that you sell to a consumer is for one cup of tea. The tea bag you'd sell to a restaurant might be for a whole jug of tea.

"The taste could be slightly different as well. For example, you may sell a very spicy product, but the restaurant doesn't want a spicy product; its clientele prefers milder tastes. Sometimes you can accommodate them, sometimes you can't, depending on how many other restaurants are in the same boat.

"Another function is marketing. Marketing is pricing, packaging, and developing the particular product you're going to advertise, promote, and sell. You advertise in the trade journals to let customers know you're going to be offering a particular product.

"Marketing also includes sales. We worked as part of a team. We had a finance person, for example, who told us if we were making money or not or what kind of prices we needed in order to profit on something. This position often holds a profit responsibility. If he spends too much money, the business will lose money and he's the guy who will go out the door.

"The sales guys, although responsible for sales volume and reaching a quota every week, do not have any profit responsibility and they are always asking for lower prices, more advertising, and more promotion. The marketing guy says 'You can't have that much because if we spend that much and price the product ten cents a case less, we're going to lose money.' Marketing and sales are often at odds with each other. At budget time, there is always a battle.

"I had many businesses I was responsible for. My particular job encompassed the Good Humor business and some other odds and ends. The ice cream business is enormous and very important within Lipton. We also had a little Mideast business called Sahadi that sold fruit rolls and other products to restaurants in areas with a high concentration of Middle Eastern people. Lipton also has a dry soup business, Wishbone salad dressing, and noodles-and-sauce and rice-and-sauce businesses. Sometimes we could get these sold through restaurants if they didn't want to make the products themselves. Most restaurants like to make their own pasta, but some don't.

"I had a person I supervised who managed the day to day of the food service end and his job was to decide what pricing promotions and advertising were needed that month to sell the product. He also decided how many salespeople he needed, what kind of training they should have, where they should be stationed, which accounts they would call on, and how much time they could give to each account.

"Food service salespeople cover a lot more territory than the retail sales end. The volume is generally lower, so you can't afford to have too many salespeople.

"There's a lot of automobile travel and a very tough schedule. Sometimes the accounts will see you when you want to see them; sometimes you have to wait and see them another day and here you are, having traveled three hundred miles. So what are you going to do if you don't have it planned to see other accounts in that area? There's a lot of planning and time away from home. It affects family life very negatively.

"The sales manager has to go out and see the sales reps because they can't afford to take the time to come to you and lose sales. So, the sales manager is out in the field too, making calls and making sure the reps are using the right techniques and handling each situation the way it should be handled in order to get the maximum sales volume.

"A step up from that, in marketing, your traveling would be a lot less. The sales manager would normally report to the vice president of marketing.

"Although marketing is a step up from sales, there's a downside to it. If marketing managers are not making the expected profit, they can lose their jobs. They have the same sales volume responsibility that the salespeople have because the salespeople report to them.

"They make an agreement with sales—they say, for example, 'Okay, we're going to sell a hundred units of X to Denny's.' Now say they only sell ninety units. The sales guy has the first responsibility and the marketing person does too, having agreed that a hundred units was what could be sold with the certain advertising, price, and quality of the product. But he missed it, so he's also on the line.

"This business is extraordinarily time-consuming. It never ends. No marketing job in today's environment is nine to five. There is always competition.

"The upside is that most successful salespeople like their jobs. You have to like it. If you don't like walking in and talking to people every day, this job isn't for you.

"There's a lot of schmoozing that goes on. You get to know the purchasing person, and if you've been calling on him for a number of years, theoretically, you'd better get to know who his wife is and who the kids are and when their birthdays are and take him out to dinner. You're not giving expensive presents—those are out—but little courtesies are okay.

"The money is no better than it is in retail. I wouldn't say that the money is terrific. It's hard work, and you're not going to end up being wealthy. But you get a good pension plan and you get bonuses. There are a lot of incentives: trips, prizes, and cash.

"When you're selling food, you're selling the brand name or a recipe. You're not selling what it can do—you're selling recognition. You might cook up a batch of macaroni and cheese for the purchaser to sample, but it's not the same as selling a computer or a car. You don't have to know how to cook. So you say, 'I don't know how to cook, but the directions here are so simple even I can do this. Just give me a pot and water and I'll show you.' If you're selling a car, you have to know all the features the car has. It's much more complex. Food service is much simpler in some ways."

Advice from Chris Fuller

"The most important thing is that you have to like traveling and meeting people and talking to people every day. You have to be able to follow directions. You're going to have a regional manager or a division manager over you who will be giving you directions, and you will have to follow those directions explicitly.

"What you do every day is tracked—where you have been, who you have seen, and what you have sold. Every day. You are in a fish bowl. Every salesperson in the United States has got his or her working life on a computer somewhere.

"You need to be a gregarious person, and you have to be thick-skinned and able to take criticism. You can get a lot of complaints from a customer. A shipment didn't come in on time. Or he thinks he was shorted, or the macaroni and cheese didn't taste the same as the batch you cooked up for him that day. Are you sure it's the same product? All that kind of thing. There's constant haranguing. The purchasing agent you're dealing with has been criticized by his boss and the first guy that's going to walk through that door—you—is going to get it.

"If you go into food service, in order to advance you might want to move over to the retail side at a later date, selling to supermarkets. Your eventual aim is to go up the ladder in sales and then go into marketing. A lot of people from sales go into marketing. You need to start young, when you're in your twenties, then move over to marketing in your early thirties. If you don't move to marketing in your early thirties, it will be too late and you'll get stuck in sales. There's a corporate system you have to learn and follow.

"But it's a good career. It's a stable business. The companies that are in it are solid. They're not fly-by-night. For the most part, they're not going to go out of business.

"You have to get up and do something every day; you can't rest on your laurels. If you like people and competition, you'll be fine."

Meet Kevin Whelan— Marketing/Product Manager

Kevin Whelan has had a long, successful career in marketing. He has been with Hill-Rom, a capital equipment manufacturer based in South Carolina, since 1995. He earned his M.B.A. in 1982 from Georgia State University in Atlanta.

How Kevin Whelan Got Started

"I went to Spring Hill College in Mobile, Alabama, and graduated with a B.A. in history in 1978. I was then an army officer for four years. In 1982, I left the army and looked for a job where I could be involved in activities that would allow me to measure the results of my actions. I wanted to be involved in some sort of free-enterprise business.

"I went to work for a company called American Hospital Supply as a logistics specialist. That had been my specialty in the army. Logistics is the movement of materials through distribution to some end point. In the case of American Hospital Supply, the end point was a hospital customer.

"I was there two years, and in my second year I was approached to consider going into sales at the same company. I sold a variety of hospital supplies for one year. After one year that company was reorganizing and I was part of a reduction in force. In other words, I was canned.

"I enjoyed the job but I did it very poorly. My first foray into sales was a disaster. I never asked people to buy anything. I would call on a hospital and show them my products. I'd ask them if they liked the products, if they liked my company, and if they liked me. And they'd always answer yes, but I never asked for the order. So getting laid off was not a surprise. I was losing money for them.

"The one attribute I did have was that I had strong relationships with customers. One of my customers was approached by another of her sales reps who worked for Kimberly-Clark and asked if she knew anyone who might be interested in selling for them in the Baltimore area. I had been in Richmond, Virginia, at the time.

"She gave my name and I was hired. I was with Kimberly-Clark a total of ten years. The first five years were in sales and I sold in three different territories: Baltimore, Pittsburgh, and Columbus, Ohio. Kimberly-Clark gave me the training I needed. They told me to ask for the order.

"After five years I was approached by the sales manager and asked if I would consider a job in product management. The rest is history. I had gone through the various stepping stones in sales—I was a senior sales rep involved with training—and I was also taking some business courses at Ohio State University at night. I was being considered for promotion into sales management, which would have been the next step. We had a marketing staff that had very little sales background, very little customer understanding. The sales manager thought I might be interested in moving into marketing to bring a sales perspective to that area.

"I stayed there for another five years. I started in marketing as an assistant product manager and left as product manager.

"Then I came to Hill-Rom as marketing manager in 1995. The move was prompted by my concern for a failing market in surgical products and the entire acute-care business. Hill-Rom was following the health-care market to where it was going, into long-term care and home care. I liked being in health-care marketing, but I needed to follow the patient, and Kimberly-Clark wasn't showing signs that it was going to do that as part of its long-term plans. Hill-Rom approached me through a headhunter."

Kevin Whelan—on the Job

"We manufacture, distribute, and service health-care sleeping surfaces. This is more than just hospital beds. The term *health care* includes long-term care and home care as well as hospitals. *Sleeping surfaces* covers more than just beds. For example, there are sleeping surfaces that are used to heal skin ulcers.

"A lot of people think that marketing and sales are the same thing. Salespeople try to get rid of what they have. In contrast, marketers try to get what they can get rid of. That was a corrupted quote by Ted Levitt, a marketing professor at Harvard. He said it in terms of sales companies versus marketing companies. But what the marketer does is start at the beginning of the cycle and look at the customer and say, 'Gee, I wonder what they need.' Having determined what the market needs, you then take a look at your company and try to determine if this is something you can produce for the customer. Do we know how to produce it and can we make money doing it?

"At that point we start interfacing with the product development people, who in some industries might be scientists; in my industry, it's engineers. We form a team of people—myself, the vice president of marketing, marketing researchers, engineers, advertisers, a financial advisor, and eventually salespeople—who say, 'This is something our customers really want. What can we do to meet their needs?' This is the process of idea generation. The ideas might come from talking to the customers, something we saw in a magazine, or just being out in the marketplace.

"It's a lot of pleading and cajoling and trying to convince others. And when you're trying to find out what the customers need, there's a whole group of skills that revolve around what we call market research. You might set up focus groups, bringing a group of customers together and talking to them, finding out what isn't working in their present environment. And that would bubble forth a need.

"After you do that, you want to quantify that need in the marketplace. Maybe thirty people have told you they need a particular device, but I'm not going to build that product for thirty people. I want to make sure there are enough people out there who are willing to buy such a thing. You do another set of research—this I coordinate with a researcher.

"Concept development is the next step in the process. This is where you develop a word or paragraph that describes the device. You take that to engineers who will develop a prototype. In our case, they'll make a bed.

"You then take this bed to the marketplace. This is called the alpha site test. It gets shipped to three or four nursing homes or other health-care facilities and often I get on a plane and meet up with it at the end destination. You don't put anybody on this bed; it's not necessarily safe at this point; you just show it to customers—in our case that would most likely be the nurses—and ask them to evaluate it.

"You go into a little circle, then, of building and taking it out, building and taking it out. Each time you do that, you learn something new. We're trying to improve the product based on the suggestions we get.

"Once you are 95 percent sure this is the product you want, you take it to one big final test that's called the beta site test. Here you have a patient use the bed. After you deliver the product you leave and see if the product will work without your standing there. Later you go back and interview the nurses to see if they are happy with it. The beta site test gives you a go, or a no go.

"Concurrently with this you put the bed through other testing—safety checks, for example, to make sure it meets FDA guidelines. We also test for claims. For example, at some point in the future I might want to be able to say, 'If you buy this bed, you will get great healing of skin sores.' I need to be able to document that claim.

"If it's a go, the engineers start figuring out how to mass produce it and I figure out how we can make money on it. For that I have to look at the cost and how much people are willing to pay for it. One of the big misconceptions in this business is that you take the cost and add something to it. Price is not determined that way; it's determined by what people are willing to pay. Once I have done that, I take it to the vice president of marketing for approval.

"Then we start making them and I go into the promotion-planning stage. Now that I have a product, I have to find a way of getting the word out. I'll make brochures and do the advertising. This is all part of my job. I also come up with ways to teach salespeople what to say about it. At the same time I'm crunching a lot of numbers, looking to see how fast the product will be made, how fast we can get out to the field, how many will be bought, and what our projection is for making money.

"Once I'm able to set a date for introducing this product, we hold big sales meetings and tell the reps how to sell it, why they should sell it, and send them loose.

"Then I monitor the product to see if it's meeting its sale projections. If I'm not making those numbers, my boss, the vice president of marketing, wants to know why and what I'm going to do about it. If I am making the numbers or doing better, he wants to know why and why I'm not selling more. There's no winning in this business.

"Then I'm still following up with customers—is it still meeting their needs and if not, what changes do we have to make? I also follow up with the salespeople, determining what else they need to sell the product. And with the engineers, I ask, 'Is the price right? How can we manufacture this and get the cost down?'

"In a typical day, week, or month, you're constantly pushing every bit and piece of this process along—no two days are alike. The process takes anywhere from a year to five years.

"I put in probably about fifty hours a week, basically Monday through Friday, eight to six. There's also travel involved; maybe 25 percent of my time is traveling.

"I don't choose to make it a stressful job, but it could be stressful for some people, and there are stressful times. If we're introducing a product that's not going well and sales are plummeting and we can't figure out why, it can be very stressful. In a long-term sense, my job is on the line. If sales are down on any given day, then I wouldn't be fired, but if I can't meet our profit goals over a one- to two-year period, I'd be replaced.

"What I like most is the number of different things I get to do. My job is to influence a lot of different people, and the best way to do that is talk in their language. I have to be able to talk accounting to accountants, advertising to advertisers, patient care to nurses, sales techniques to the sales staff, engineering to our engineers, business management to the vice president of my company. No two conversations are alike.

"I'm paid a salary and a bonus based on the performance of the products I'm managing. The salary range for people in my type of job is $70,000 to $90,000 a year, including the bonus.

"The biggest downside is that I support people—the salespeople—who are making more money than I am. A lot more money. But for me, marketing is more fun than sales."

Some Advice from Kevin Whelan

"The best marketers have a dual background. They have been salespeople and they also have the formal education—they have an M.B.A. My preference is to get an M.B.A. the way I did. After you've been in sales for a while, then go back and get it."

Meet Ernie Stetenfeld— Public Relations Director

Ernie Stetenfeld has been with AAA Wisconsin since 1987. He started in a general capacity, then worked his way up to his current position as public relations director. He earned his master's degree in journalism and mass communications at Drake University in Des Moines, Iowa, in 1982.

How Ernie Stetenfeld Got Started

"I got into this by virtue of having garnered some expertise in the magazine end of the spectrum. My undergraduate degree is in religion and anthropology from Northwestern in 1979. My graduate degree is in journalism and mass communications with two emphases. One was news editorial and the other was magazine journalism. My first job was as a newspaper reporter and then shortly after that I started up a trade journal in Chicago for the multihousing industry. I enjoy magazine work, and I was hired initially at AAA because of that experience. I had also done other forms of public relations and government relations in the interim as well."

Ernie Stetenfeld—on the Job

"I have five major areas of purview: member relations, which is mostly a complaint-solving activity; general public relations, including news bureau activity and media relations; traffic safety promotion, which has been an AAA interest from our founding in 1902; member magazine production—until about a year ago I was editor, now I'm executive editor; and government relations and lobbying.

"I have three professional-level staff people—one who serves as an editor, one who serves primarily as public relations and media relations manager, and another who is member relations manager. There are two and a half support staff positions and, working for the member relations manager—we have a club of about half a million members—are six full-time employees and three part-time people.

"In the member relations area, we have direct sales goals. The people who work in that area serve as the inbound telemarketing staff for AAA Wisconsin. So if a potential member calls our toll-free number, for example, our staff will try to convince the caller that joining AAA is a good idea.

"Indirectly, and more generally—and probably more importantly—my department serves in a marketing support capacity. We're the people who garner the free publicity for AAA in Wisconsin. We serve in a media relations capacity and are out to get the good name and logo of AAA into news media across the state, a) for public information, and b) to soften the market for our marketing purposes. Our goal is to further entrench the AAA name, logo, and reputation among the general public and our member base in the state. The purpose of this is to help them to think of us in a good way when we send them some sort of marketing pitch, such as for insurance, or travel agency products, or other membership products.

"We want to create an environment for AAA in the state that disposes the general public and members to think well of us in terms of reputation and, as a result of that, to be receptive to our attempts to market products and services.

"In a typical day I might talk with one or two members and give a few media interviews, although I give only about 30 percent of the interviews—the media relations manager does more. I might write a piece of testimony for public policy purposes, for instance, to influence legislation on the state level. I might help edit a magazine article or write a short article for our bimonthly member publication. But I would spend probably most of my time in meetings with other department heads, trying to coordinate the activities of our various business units and do any necessary troubleshooting. In fact, today, which is a rather atypical day, 90 percent of my time has been spent troubleshooting. We recently have undergone a merger—AAA Wisconsin and AAA Michigan have joined forces—and so there are a number of things, system changes, for example, that necessitate more of my time being spent on troubleshooting than might normally be the case. If something is related to an AAA stance on public policy and we get a question about it and need to make an announcement about it, that would tend to be in my area as well.

"I don't normally think of my job as more promotion than public relations, but there is a definite promotion component to it.

"I've always enjoyed magazine and publications work and I like editing, and that is the area I probably enjoy most. I also enjoy doing interviews, particularly for radio.

"The government relations aspect of my work probably is what I enjoy the least. Sometimes the intricacies of government relations are so arcane or convoluted, and that can lead to a sense of frustration. On both the state and federal levels, AAA does, to some extent on selected issues, try to influence public policy, especially as it relates to motorists or other travelers. For example, we recently testified before a state senate committee in favor of legislation that would outlaw children under sixteen riding in truck beds. We've had some deaths as a result of that sort of thing and that's the kind of issue AAA would back from a safety concern standpoint. I also work to track and occasionally provide AAA's input on major transportation policy in the state or even at the federal level, such as our state transportation budget, which spent almost all of 1995 getting passed.

"Salary-wise I started out at $24,000 and now earn in the high fifties. My job tends to be Monday through Friday with six or seven weekends throughout the year that I either travel or work here or at home. I probably work an average of fifty-five hours a week—it used to be longer. I was able to add another position in my department, so that has freed me up significantly."

Advice from Ernie Stetenfeld

"In a PR type of job, don't expect to end up just doing one thing. In most instances, you'll be called on to relate to any number of different publics and to use any number of different communications tools, so it's best to broaden your arsenal."

Salaries for Corporate Managers

According to a National Association of Colleges and Employers survey, starting salary offers to marketing majors graduating in 1995 averaged about $25,000; advertising majors, about $22,000. The median annual salary of marketing, advertising, and public relations managers was $44,000 in 1994. The lowest 10 percent earned $21,000 or less, while the top 10 percent earned $98,000 or more.

Many managers earn bonuses equal to 10 percent or more of their salaries. Surveys show that salary levels vary substantially depending upon the level of managerial responsibility, length of service, education, and the employer's size, location, and industry. For example, manufacturing firms generally pay marketing, advertising, and public relations managers higher salaries than nonmanufacturing firms. For sales managers, the size of their sales territory is another important factor.

According to a 1994 survey by Abbot, Langer and Associates, of Crete, Illinois, annual incomes for sales/marketing managers varied greatly, from under $28,000 to more than $250,000, depending on the manager's level of education, experience, industry, and the number of employees he or she supervises.

The median annual income for each position was as follows:

Advertising managers	$44,000
Chief marketing executives	$69,000
Market research managers	$59,000
Product/brand managers	$57,000
Regional sales managers	$69,000
Sales promotion managers	$45,000

Other surveys show a range from $44,000 to $145,000.

CHAPTER SIX

Engineering Managers

E ngineering managers plan, coordinate, and direct
research, development, design, production, and
computer-related activities. They supervise a staff that
may include engineers, scientists, and technicians, along with
support personnel.

Engineering managers determine technical goals within
broad outlines provided by top management. These goals may
include the redesign of an industrial machine or improvements
in manufacturing processes.

Managers make detailed plans for the accomplishment of
these goals. For example, they may develop the overall concepts
of new products or identify problems standing in the way of
project completion. They forecast costs and equipment and
personnel needs for projects and programs. They hire and assign engineers, technicians, computer specialists, and support
personnel to carry out specific parts of the projects, then supervise their work and review their designs, programs, and reports.

Managers coordinate the activities of their unit with other
units or organizations. They confer with higher levels of management; with financial, industrial production, marketing, and
other managers; and with contractors and equipment suppliers.
They also establish working and administrative procedures and
policies.

Engineering managers direct and coordinate production,
operations, quality assurance, testing, or maintenance in industrial plants; or they plan and coordinate the design and development of machinery, products, systems, and processes. Many

are plant engineers who direct and coordinate the maintenance, operation, design, and installation of equipment and machinery in industrial plants. Others manage research and development activities that produce new products and processes or improve existing ones.

Some engineering processing managers head sections of perhaps three to ten or more engineers or other professionals. Above them are heads of divisions, composed of a number of sections, with as many as fifteen to fifty engineers. A few are directors of research or of large laboratories.

Engineering managers spend most of their time in an office. Some managers, however, may also work in laboratories or industrial plants, where they normally are exposed to the same conditions as research scientists or as production workers. Most work at least forty hours a week and may work much longer on occasion to meet project deadlines. Some may experience considerable pressure to meet technical goals within a short time or within a tight budget.

Some engineers work in engineering management or in sales, where an engineering background enables them to discuss the technical aspects of a product and assist in planning its installation or use.

Training for Engineers

Bachelor's degrees in engineering from accredited engineering programs are usually required for beginning engineering jobs. College graduates with degrees in physical science or mathematics may occasionally qualify for some engineering jobs, primarily in engineering specialties in high demand. Most engineering degrees are granted in branches such as electrical, mechanical, or civil engineering. However, engineers trained in one branch may work in another. This flexibility allows employers to meet staffing needs in new technologies and specialties in short supply. It also allows engineers to shift to fields with better employment prospects, or ones that match their interests more closely.

In addition to the standard engineering degree, many colleges offer degrees in engineering technology in either two- or four-year programs. These programs prepare students for practical design and production work rather than for jobs that require more theoretical, scientific, and mathematical knowledge. Graduates of four-year technology programs may get jobs similar to those obtained by graduates with bachelor's degrees in engineering. In fact, some employers regard them as having skills between those of a technician and an engineer.

Graduate training is essential for engineering faculty positions but is not required for the majority of entry-level engineering jobs. Many engineers obtain master's degrees to learn new technology, to broaden their education, and to enhance promotion opportunities.

Nearly 340 colleges and universities offer bachelor's degrees in engineering, and nearly 300 colleges offer bachelor's degrees in engineering technology, although not all are accredited programs. Most institutions offer programs in the larger branches of engineering—e.g., civil, mechanical, electrical—but only a few offer some of the smaller specialties, such as transportation or marine engineering.

Also, programs of the same title may vary in content. For example, some emphasize industrial practices, preparing students for a job in industry, while others are more theoretical and are better for students preparing to take graduate work. Therefore, students should investigate curriculums and check accreditations carefully before selecting a college. Admissions requirements for undergraduate engineering schools include courses in advanced high school mathematics and the physical sciences.

Bachelor's degree programs in engineering are typically designed to last four years, but many students find that it takes between four and five years to complete their studies. In a typical four-year college curriculum, the first two years are spent studying basic sciences (mathematics, physics, and chemistry), introductory engineering, and the humanities, social sciences, and English. In the last two years, most courses are in engineering, usually with a concentration in one branch. For example, the last two years of an aerospace program might include courses such as fluid mechanics, heat transfer, applied aerodynamics, analytical mechanics, flight vehicle design, trajectory dynamics, and aerospace propulsion systems. Some programs offer a general engineering curriculum; students then specialize in graduate school or on the job.

A few engineering schools and two-year colleges have agreements whereby the two-year college provides the initial engineering education and the engineering school automatically admits students for their last two years. In addition, a few engineering schools have arrangements whereby students spend three years in a liberal arts college studying pre-engineering subjects and two years in the engineering school and receive bachelor's degrees from each. Some colleges and universities offer fifth-year master's degree programs.

Some five- or even six-year cooperative plans combine classroom study and practical work, permitting students to gain valuable experience and finance part of their education on the job.

Registration

All fifty states and the District of Columbia require registration for engineers whose work may affect life, health, or property, or who offer their services to the public. In 1992, nearly 380,000 engineers were registered. Registration generally requires a degree from an engineering program accredited by the Accreditation Board for Engineering and Technology, four years of relevant work experience, and successful completion of a state examination. Some states will not register people with degrees in engineering technology.

The Qualities You'll Need

Engineers should be able to work as part of a team and should have creativity, an analytical mind, and a capacity for detail. In addition, engineers should be able to express themselves well both orally and in writing.

Getting Ahead

Beginning engineering graduates usually do routine work under the supervision of experienced engineers and, in larger companies, may also receive formal classroom or seminar-type training. As they gain knowledge and experience, they are assigned more difficult tasks with greater independence to develop designs, solve problems, and make decisions.

Engineers may become technical specialists or may supervise a staff or team of engineers and technicians. Some eventually become engineering managers or enter other managerial, management support, or sales jobs.

Some engineers obtain graduate degrees in engineering or business administration to improve advancement opportunities; others obtain law degrees and become patent attorneys. Many high-level executives in government and industry began their careers as engineers.

Training for Engineering Managers

Experience as an engineer is the usual requirement for becoming an engineering manager. Consequently, educational requirements are similar to those for engineering professionals.

Engineering managers start as engineers. Bachelor's degrees in engineering from accredited engineering programs are acceptable for beginning engineering jobs, but many engineers increase their chances for promotion to manager by obtaining master's degrees in engineering or business administration. A degree in business administration or engineering management is especially useful for becoming a general manager.

In addition to educational requirements, engineers generally must have demonstrated above-average technical skills to be considered for promotion to manager. Superiors also look for leadership and communication skills, as well as managerial attributes such as the ability to make rational decisions, to manage time well, to organize and coordinate work effectively, to establish good working and personal relationships, and to motivate others. Also, a successful manager must have the desire to manage. Many engineers want to be promoted but actually prefer doing technical work.

Employment Figures

Although engineering managers are found in almost all industries, nearly two-fifths are employed in manufacturing, especially in the industrial machinery and equipment, electrical and electronic equipment, transportation equipment, instruments, and chemicals industries. They also work for engineering, management, and computer services companies.

Others work for government, colleges and universities, and nonprofit research organizations. The majority of these manage industrial research, development, and design projects.

Looking Ahead

Employment of engineering managers is expected to increase faster than the average for all occupations through the year 2005. Opportunities for those who wish to become engineering managers should be closely related to the growth of the occupations they supervise and the industries in which they are found.

Underlying much of the growth for managers in science and engineering are competitive pressures and advancing technologies that force companies to update and improve products more frequently. Research and investment in plants and equipment to expand output of goods and services and to raise productivity also will add to employment requirements for engineering managers involved in research and development, design, and the operation and maintenance of production facilities.

Many of the industries that employ engineers derive a large portion of their business from defense contracts. Because defense expenditures are being reduced, employment growth and job outlook for managers in these industries may not be as strong in the future as in the 1980s, when defense expenditures were increasing.

Despite growth in employment, most job openings will result from the need to replace workers who leave the occupation. Because many engineers are eligible for management positions and seek promotion, competition can be stiff for these openings.

What It's Really Like

Meet George Ragsdale— Engineering Manager/Attorney

George Ragsdale is vice president of Simons Engineering, an engineering/design firm located in Atlanta, Georgia. In 1973 he graduated from Cornell University in Ithaca, New York, with a B.S. in chemical engineering. He later received a J.D. degree in 1992 and an M.B.A. in 1993, both from Widener University in Wilmington, Delaware.

How George Ragsdale Got Started

"I started working in the engineering field immediately upon graduation from Cornell in 1973 and began the practice of law immediately upon passing the Pennsylvania Bar in 1992.

"I wanted to be a chemical engineer from the time I was in the fourth grade. I always loved chemistry and math as a child and thought that the chemical engineering field would be very challenging and interesting to me.

"Later, as my roles shifted from actually performing engineering projects to managing an engineering department, I found myself not as fulfilled as when I first began engineering work. Plus, I had always had a love for the law, and a lot of people, primarily my wife, encouraged me to go to law school.

"After graduating from law school, I continued to manage an engineering department full-time and began a family law practice on a part-time basis. Then, an opportunity arose to combine both my legal training and my engineering background and I jumped at the chance."

George Ragsdale—on the Job

"I am a senior staff manager of our design engineering firm. Right now, I supervise fifteen accountants, seven human resource professionals, and a secretary. One of the things I really enjoy about my current role is that every day is both different and unpredictable. Every day is a mixture of reviewing project performance, reviewing client contracts, and a lot of other things. Aside from being general counsel for our firm, I also manage the accounting, finance, and human resources functions. Each of these disciplines has its own unique challenges that are collectively guaranteed to keep each day interesting.

"I generally work about ten to eleven hours a day, four days a week and six hours on Fridays. I also take work home with me almost every night, but try not to do so on the weekends. There is really no such thing as a typical day. Each day is different and that is the way I like it. It is not really stressful (to me) but is very demanding. I spend about 20 percent of my time on the phone, primarily with other attorneys, another 40 percent of my time in meetings or discussions face-to-face, and the remaining 20 percent doing paperwork, primarily contract reviews.

"I consider the real upside of my job to be the opportunity to continue to learn while working at something I enjoy. Because my legal training and experience were quite narrow when I began this job, there are a lot of opportunities for me to become proficient in other areas of the law and rely less on outside counsel for assistance. The downside is that I personally have a tendency to try to do it all. And, on occasion, I overcommit because I really love what I am doing—almost too much!"

Advice from George Ragsdale

"For anyone who has similar interests to mine—both law and engineering—I recommend some practical experience in the engineering field first. I would also advise that in whatever field you may want to practice law, firsthand experience with the 'operation' of that field of work provides a tremendous advantage in the legal profession over others who may not have had that practical experience."

Salaries

Earnings for Engineers

Starting salaries for engineers with bachelor's degrees are significantly higher than starting salaries of bachelor's degree graduates in other fields. According to the National Association of Colleges and Employers, engineering graduates with bachelor's degrees averaged about $34,100 a year in private industry in 1994; those with master's degrees and no experience, $40,200 a year; and those with doctorates, $55,300.

For those with bachelor's degrees, starting salaries vary by branch, as shown below:

Aerospace	$30,860
Chemical	$39,204
Civil	$29,809
Electrical	$34,840
Industrial	$33,267
Materials	$33,429
Mechanical	$35,051
Mining	$32,638
Nuclear	$33,603
Petroleum	$38,286

A survey of workplaces in 160 metropolitan areas reported that beginning engineers had median annual earnings of about $33,900 in 1993, with the middle half earning between about $30,900 and $36,900 a year. In 1995, median salaries for the following engineering specialties were:

Aerospace	$50,200
Chemical	$53,100
Civil	$44,700
Electrical	$48,000
Industrial	$49,000
Mechanical	$46,400

The average annual salary for engineers in the federal government in nonsupervisory, supervisory, and managerial positions was $58,080 in 1995. Experienced midlevel engineers with no supervisory responsibilities had median annual earnings of about $54,400, with the middle half earning between about $49,800 and $59,600 a year.

Earnings for Engineering Managers

Earnings for engineering managers vary by specialty and level of management. Science and engineering managers had average salaries that ranged from $50,000 to well over $100,000 for the most senior managers in large organizations, according to the limited data available.

Managers often earn about 15 to 25 percent more than those they directly supervise, although there are cases where some employees are paid more than the manager who supervises them, especially in research.

In addition, engineering managers, especially those at higher levels, often are provided more benefits than nonmanagerial workers in their organizations. Higher-level managers often are provided with expense accounts, stock option plans, and bonuses.

CHAPTER SEVEN

Restaurant and Hotel Managers

Restaurant Management

Eating places range from restaurants that serve fast food or that emphasize elegant dining to institutional dining in school and employee cafeterias, hospitals, and nursing facilities. The cuisine offered, its price, and the setting in which it is consumed vary greatly, but the employees of these diverse dining facilities have many responsibilities in common.

Efficient and profitable operation of restaurants and institutional food service facilities requires that managers and assistant managers select and appropriately price interesting menu items, efficiently use food and other supplies, achieve consistent quality in food preparation and service, recruit and train adequate numbers of workers and supervise their work, and attend to the various administrative aspects of the business.

Restaurant Managers

In most restaurants, the manager is assisted by one or more assistant managers, depending on the size and business hours of the establishment. In large establishments, as well as in many others that offer fine dining, the management team consists of a general manager, one or more assistant managers, and an executive chef. In fast-food restaurants and other food service facilities that operate long hours, seven days a week, the manager is aided by several assistant managers, each of whom supervises a shift of workers.

Managers interview, hire, and, when necessary, discharge workers. They familiarize newly hired workers with the establishment's policies and practices and oversee their training. Managers schedule the work hours of employees, ensuring that there are enough workers present during busy periods, but not too many during slow periods.

Restaurant and food service managers supervise the kitchen and the dining room. They oversee food preparation and cooking, checking the quality of the food and the sizes of portions to ensure that dishes are prepared and garnished correctly and in a timely manner. They also investigate and resolve customers' complaints about food quality or service. During busy periods, managers may roll up their sleeves and help with the cooking, clearing of tables, or other tasks. They direct the cleaning of the kitchen and dining areas and the washing of tableware, kitchen utensils, and equipment to maintain company and government sanitation standards. They monitor workers and observe patrons on a continual basis to ensure compliance with health and safety standards and local liquor regulations.

Managers have a variety of administrative responsibilities. In larger establishments, much of this work is delegated to a bookkeeper, but in others, managers must keep accurate records of the hours and wages of employees, prepare the payroll, and do paperwork to comply with licensing laws and reporting requirements of tax, wage and hour, unemployment compensation, and Social Security laws. They also must maintain records of the costs of supplies and equipment purchased and ensure that accounts with suppliers are paid on a regular basis. In addition, managers record the number, type, and cost of items sold to weed out dishes that are unpopular or less profitable. Many managers are able to ease the burden of record keeping and paperwork through the use of computers.

Managers are among the first to arrive and the last to leave at night. At the conclusion of each day, or sometimes each shift, managers must tally the cash received and charge receipts and balance them against the record of sales. They are responsible for depositing the day's income at the bank or securing it in a safe place. Managers are also responsible for checking that ovens, grills, and lights are off, doors are locked, and alarm systems are activated. Ordering supplies and dealing with suppliers are important aspects of restaurant and food service managers' responsibilities.

Executive Chefs

The executive chef is responsible for the operation of the kitchen, while the assistant managers oversee service in the dining room and other areas of the operation. In some smaller restaurants, the executive chef may also be the general manager and sometimes an owner.

Training for Restaurant and Food Service Managers

Many restaurant and food service manager positions are filled by promoting experienced food and beverage preparation and service workers. Waiters, waitresses, chefs, and fast-food workers who have demonstrated their potential for handling increased responsibility sometimes advance to assistant manager or management trainee jobs when openings occur.

Executive chefs need extensive experience working as chefs, and general managers need experience working as assistant managers. However, most food service management companies and national or regional restaurant chains also recruit management trainees from among the graduates of two- and four-year college programs. Food service and restaurant chains prefer to hire graduates with degrees in restaurant and institutional food service management, but they often hire individuals with degrees in other fields who have demonstrated interest and aptitude.

A bachelor's degree in restaurant and food service management provides a particularly strong preparation for a career in this occupation. In 1993, more than 160 colleges and universities offered four-year programs in restaurant and hotel management or institutional food service management. For those who do not want to pursue a four-year degree, a good alternative is provided by the more than 800 community and junior colleges, technical institutes, and other institutions that offer programs in these fields leading to associate's degrees or other formal certificates.

Both two-year and four-year programs provide instruction in subjects such as accounting, business law and management, food planning and preparation, and nutrition. Some programs combine classroom and laboratory study with internships that provide on-the-job experience. In addition, many educational institutions offer culinary programs that provide food preparation training, which can lead to a career as a cook or chef and provide a foundation for advancement to an executive chef position.

Most restaurant chains and food service management companies have rigorous training programs for management jobs. Through a combination of classroom and on-the-job training, trainees receive instruction and gain work experience in all aspects of the operations of a restaurant or institutional food service facility: food preparation, nutrition, sanitation, security, company policies and procedures, personnel management, record keeping, and preparation of reports. Usually after six months or a year, trainees receive their first permanent assignments as assistant managers.

A measure of professional achievement for restaurant and food service managers is earning the designation of Certified Foodservice Management Professional (FMP). Although not a requirement for employment or advancement in the occupation, voluntary certification provides recognition of professional competence, particularly for managers who acquired their skills largely on the job. The Educational Foundation of the National Restaurant Association awards the FMP designation to managers who achieve a qualifying score on a written examination, complete a series of courses that cover a range of food service management topics, and who meet standards of work experience in the field.

Looking Ahead

Restaurant and Food Service Managers

Employment of restaurant and food service managers is expected to increase much faster than the average for all occupations through the year 2005. In addition to growth in demand for these managers, the need to replace managers who transfer to other occupations or stop working will create many job openings. Job opportunities are expected to be best for persons with bachelor's or associate's degrees in restaurant and institutional food service management.

Employment growth is expected to vary by industry. Eating and drinking places will provide the most new jobs as the number of establishments increases and other industries continue to contract out their food services. Population growth, rising personal incomes, and increased leisure time will continue to produce growth in the number of meals consumed outside the home. To meet the demand for prepared food, more restaurants will be built, and more managers will be employed to supervise them. In addition, the number of managerial jobs will increase as schools, hospitals, and other businesses contract out more of their food services to institutional food service companies.

Employment of wage and salary managers in eating and drinking places is expected to increase more rapidly than self-employed managers. New restaurants are increasingly af-filiated with national chains rather than being independently owned and operated. As this trend continues, fewer owners will manage restaurants themselves, and more restaurant managers will be employed to run the establishments.

Employment in eating and drinking establishments is not very sensitive to changes in economic conditions, so restaurant and food service managers are rarely laid off during hard times. However, competition among restaurants is always intense, and many restaurants do not survive.

What It's Really Like

Meet Linda Dickinson—Chef and Menu Planner at Moosewood Restaurant

Moosewood Restaurant in Ithaca, New York, opened its doors in 1973 as a collectively run vegetarian eating establishment. Part of the counterculture at the time, Moosewood workers were early adherents to the now-popular philosophy that food could be healthful and taste good at the same time. They also felt that the workplace should be a fun place to be, with all business decisions made jointly.

Moosewood is not operated along the lines of traditional restaurants. At present, eighteen women and men rotate through the jobs necessary to make a restaurant go, such as planning menus, preparing and serving food, setting long-term goals—and washing pots. Their ranks are bolstered by about half a dozen regular employees. Most of the Moosewood collective members have worked together for over ten years, several since the restaurant's early days.

Moosewood was at first known only locally. Now, two decades and several highly acclaimed cookbooks later, Moosewood's reputation for serving fine food in a friendly atmosphere has spread nationally.

Linda Dickinson began working at Moosewood in 1973. She started as a waitress but soon took on the responsibilities of chef and menu planner. She is also coauthor of *New Recipes from Moosewood Restaurant*, *Sundays at Moosewood Restaurant*, and *Moosewood Restaurant Cooks at Home*.

Linda Dickinson—on the Job

"When we're not working on a cookbook, I put in twenty to thirty hours a week at the restaurant. When we are writing, I generally never work less than two shifts, or twelve to fourteen hours. A menu-planning week is closer to thirty or forty hours, depending on how busy we are.

"This situation is really much different than most people would encounter. Most people with a cooking position in a traditional restaurant would have to put in more hours than that. That was part of the reason Moosewood was formed as a collective. We wanted to be able to have time to do other things. Our scheduling is flexible and it varies from week to week.

"The first thing I do when I go into work is talk to the menu planner, who lets me know what is planned for the meal I'm doing. There's always at least one other cook, sometimes as many as two other cooks, depending on what season it is and how busy we're going to be.

"I consult with the other cooks, too, to see who wants to do what, so we can divide up the tasks. Then we start working. We have soups to prepare, salads, and entrees. I might have to make one soup and two entrees—it depends on how many cooks we have that day. I spend the next three hours cooking until we're open for business. Once we're open, I spend the rest of the time serving the food onto plates so the waiters can take it to the customers.

"The days I'm menu planning, I'm not cooking. I plan the menu according to the season, trying to get a balance of different dishes, some dairy with eggs and cheese, some dishes that are suitable for vegans—vegetarians who don't eat any eggs or dairy products. I want to balance the dishes according to spicy and not spicy. I also think about the weather. If it's really hot, I might offer a chilled soup and a salad plate, that sort of thing.

"I have to check to see what supplies we have on hand, what we're running low on, what we need to order. I do clean up, I put away deliveries when they come, and I take charge of the refrigerators, cleaning them out.

"I usually put the order in the night before. We have various suppliers who bring different things. So there'll be a lot of different orders that go in during the week for basic supplies, then every day we order from our produce supplier.

"Moosewood is not the normal cooking situation. We have much more freedom. In a big place, you might be doing line cooking, performing one particular task, and only that, over and over. There'd be a hierarchy to deal with, too.

"We have a much friendlier situation, which doesn't mean it's not a high-pressure job. When you're in the kitchen and it's very busy, you don't get break time. You have to stay until the food is ready and the people have been served. Many times you're on your feet all day. It's a high-intensity situation. You can be under a lot of pressure. You could run out of food in the middle of a shift and have to start making more. If you don't have enough ingredients for the same dish, you might have to change the menu if you run out. You could burn things, then have to start over.

"As in any profession, there can be tensions among coworkers, and then there's the heat in the kitchen to deal with. Even though we have air conditioning, it still gets very hot with the ovens going. If you're a cook, you have to expect to be hot a lot. We expanded the restaurant and kitchen area recently, but it's still crowded in there and hot. And it's physically demanding work, lifting heavy pots.

"But I'm happy with the niche I've found. Cooking seems more real to me than sitting in an office doing paperwork. You're producing a product, you're doing your best to make it good, and you're serving it to people who you hope will agree with your taste. You're trying to make food that looks appealing and tastes good. It's a real activity—you're taking care of a basic need in life. People need to eat. So there's the satisfaction in producing a product and having it be well received.

"In general, our group of people is pretty congenial, so you can have fun while you're working, talking with the other like-minded people. In this sort of restaurant it's like being with an extended family.

"But sometimes we get irritable customers and that can be annoying. The waiters will come back and report that someone was unhappy. I usually don't take it personally, but still, one always prefers to hear good things. But since we've been in business as long as we have and we're popular, we get much more good feedback than bad."

How Linda Dickinson Got Started

"In 1968 I got my B.A. in German literature from Harper College, which is now called SUNY Binghamton. But there were no jobs in German literature.

"Originally, I wasn't attracted to the profession—I fell into it. I waitressed at various places, then in 1973 I started at Moosewood as a waitress. The group had already opened the restaurant a couple of months earlier. As new people came in, they included them in the decision-making process.

"After I waitressed for a while at Moosewood, I told them I knew how to make curries. Because it was a very loose kind of restaurant and nobody had gone to cooking school—they were basically home cooks, not professionals—when they heard that I could make curries, they had me come into the kitchen. It was obvious I had more of an aptitude for cooking than I did for waitressing. I was attracted to cooking; I liked playing with the different seasonings. For example, with Indian food there are a lot of exotic combinations that interested me. By learning that skill on my own, it got me into the slot at Moosewood.

"In the early days, everybody who knew how to do certain dishes would teach the other cooks those dishes. I would teach other people about making curries and they would teach me their dishes. And we were all reading cookbooks and learning how to do more things on our own.

"Because our menu changes with every meal, someone has to be in charge of planning what we would have and ordering the food for us. After the first year or two it evolved that a group of menu planners was formed and I became one of them."

Advice from Linda Dickinson

"Some places won't hire you unless you have formal training, while other places would. First, try to figure out what sort of cook or chef you want to be. For some sorts, formal training is a necessity.

"The more experience you can get on your own—cooking at home, cooking for your friends, or observing a cook in your family—the more you can learn about cooking in general, the better it will be. But the fancier expensive places are going to want formal training.

"If there's a restaurant you like to go to, you like the food, you could talk to some of the people who work there or the owners to see what the requirements are.

"I'm sure there are other places, like Moosewood, that hire people not because they have some sort of formal training but because they have a feeling for food. We would consider that more important. Sometimes we have had people who've gone to culinary school and they don't work out in our kind of setting. Some of these schools are very rigid in what they teach. Things have to be done in a certain way. We don't necessarily agree with that.

"You can also take a cooking class through adult education or at a community college or with an individual who offers a course in a particular type of cooking.

"I think cooking can be a very rewarding profession. Although Moosewood isn't high paying, some other restaurants can be. And it can lead to other things, too. You could open your own restaurant or put together a cookbook. There are a lot of restaurants in the world, so there are a lot of opportunities."

Salaries for Restaurant and Food Service Managers

Median earnings for restaurant and food service managers were $421 a week in 1994. The middle 50 percent earned between about $300 and $600 a week. The lowest-paid 10 percent earned $225 a week or less, while the highest-paid 10 percent earned over $884 a week.

Earnings of restaurant and food service managers vary greatly according to their responsibilities and the type and size of establishment. Based on a survey conducted for the National Restaurant Association, the median base salary of managers in restaurants was estimated to be about $28,600 a year in 1994, but managers of the largest restaurants and institutional food service facilities often had annual salaries in excess of $45,000.

Managers of fast-food restaurants had an estimated median base salary of $25,000 a year; managers of full-menu restaurants with table service, almost $30,400; and managers of commercial and institutional cafeterias, nearly $31,400 a year in 1994.

Besides a salary, most managers received an annual bonus or incentive payment based on their performance. Most of these payments ranged between $2,000 and $8,000 a year.

Executive chefs had an estimated median base salary of about $37,000 a year in 1994, but those employed in the largest restaurants and institutional food service facilities often had base salaries over $43,000. Annual bonus or incentive payments of most executive chefs ranged between $1,500 and $6,000 a year.

The estimated median base salary of assistant managers was over $22,000 a year in 1994, but ranged from less than $19,800 in fast-food restaurants to over $25,000 in some of the largest restaurants and food service facilities. Annual bonus or incentive payments of most assistant managers ranged between $1,000 and $4,000 a year.

Manager trainees had an estimated median base salary of about $20,000 a year in 1994, with salaries of nearly $30,000 in some of the largest restaurants and food service facilities. Annual bonus or incentive payments of most trainees ranged between $500 and $2,500 a year.

Most salaried restaurant and food service managers received free meals, sick leave, health and life insurance, and one to three weeks of paid vacation a year, depending on length of service.

Hotel Management

The hotel industry is one of the largest employers in the United States. To provide an effective service to vacationers, business travelers, and local and distant enterprises needing meeting and convention space, hotels utilize the services of a variety of managers and assistants.

Hotel managers are responsible for the efficient and profitable operation of their establishments. In a small hotel, motel, or inn with a limited staff, a single manager may direct all aspects of operations. However, large hotels may employ hundreds of workers, and the manager may be aided by a number of assistant managers assigned among departments responsible for various aspects of operations. Assistant managers must see to it that the day-to-day operations of their departments meet the general manager's standards.

General Managers

The general manager has overall responsibility for the operation of the hotel. Within guidelines established by the owners of the hotel or executives of the hotel chain, the general manager sets room rates, allocates funds to departments, approves expenditures, and establishes standards for decor, housekeeping, food quality, banquet operations, and service to guests.

Resident Managers

Resident managers live in hotels and are on call twenty-four hours a day to resolve any problems or emergencies, although they normally work an eight-hour day. As the most senior assistant manager, a resident manager oversees the day-to-day operations of the hotel. In many hotels, the general manager also serves as the resident manager.

Housekeeping Managers

Executive housekeepers are responsible for ensuring that guest rooms, meeting and banquet rooms, and public areas are clean, orderly, and well maintained. They inspect rooms, order cleaning supplies, and train, schedule, and supervise the work of housekeepers.

Front Office Managers

Front office managers coordinate reservations and room assignments and train and direct the hotel's front desk staff in dealing with the public. They ensure that guests are handled courteously and efficiently, complaints and problems are resolved, and requests for special services are carried out.

Food and Beverage Managers

Food and beverage managers direct the food services of hotels. They oversee the operation of hotel restaurants, cocktail lounges, and banquet facilities. They supervise and schedule food and beverage preparation and service workers, plan menus, estimate costs, and deal with food suppliers.

Convention Managers

Convention services managers in large hotels coordinate the activities of various departments for meetings, conventions, and other special events. They meet with representatives of groups or organizations to plan the number of rooms to reserve, the desired configuration of hotel meeting spaces, and any banquet services needed. During the meeting or event, they resolve unexpected problems and monitor activities to check that hotel operations conform to the expectations of the group.

Additional Assistant Managers

Other assistant managers may be specialists responsible for activities such as personnel, accounting and office administration, marketing and sales, purchasing, security, maintenance, and recreational facilities.

Training for Hotel Personnel

With a lot of hotels, on-the-job training is possible at all levels of employment, but completing a formal training program will help you compete. Without experience, you might very well get hired, but you will likely start at the bottom of the ladder. With a college degree in hotel management or a related field, you could walk into an assistant manager position or be offered a place in a management training program.

Postsecondary training in hotel or restaurant management is preferred for most hotel management positions, although a college liberal arts degree may be sufficient when coupled with related hotel experience. In the past, most managers were promoted from the ranks of front desk clerks, housekeepers, waiters, chefs, and hotel sales workers. Although some people still advance to hotel management positions without the benefit of education or training beyond high school, postsecondary education is increasingly important.

Nevertheless, experience working in a hotel even part-time while in school is an asset to all people seeking to enter hotel management careers. Restaurant management training or experience is also a good background for entering hotel management because the success of a hotel's food service and beverage operations is often of great importance to the profitability of the entire establishment.

Bachelor's degrees in hotel and restaurant administration provide particularly strong preparation for careers in hotel management. In 1993, more than 160 colleges and universities offered bachelor's and graduate programs in this field. More than 800 community and junior colleges, technical institutes, vocational and trade schools, and other academic institutions also have programs leading to associate's degrees or other formal recognition in hotel or restaurant management. Graduates of hotel or restaurant management programs usually start as trainee assistant managers or at least advance to such positions more quickly than those without such training.

Hotel management programs usually include instruction in hotel administration, accounting, economics, marketing, housekeeping, food service management and catering, hotel maintenance engineering, and data processing, reflecting the widespread use of computers in hotel operations such as reservations, accounting, and housekeeping management. Programs encourage part-time or summer work in hotels and restaurants because the experience gained and the contacts made with employers will benefit students when they seek full-time employment after graduation.

Looking Ahead

Employment of salaried hotel managers is expected to grow about as fast as the average for all occupations through the year 2005 as more hotels and motels are built. Business travel will continue to grow, and increased domestic and foreign tourism will also create demand for additional hotels and motels.

However, manager jobs are expected to grow more slowly than the hotel industry because a growing share of the industry will be comprised of economy properties, which generally have fewer managers than full-service hotels. In the face of financial constraints, guests are becoming more bargain-conscious, and hotel chains are increasing the number of rooms in economy-class hotels. Because there are not as many departments in such hotels, fewer managers are needed on the hotel premises.

What It's Really Like

Meet LeAnne Coury— Assistant Director of Sales

LeAnne Coury has been in the hotel and sales business for twenty years. She works at the Quality Suites Hotel, a national chain. In her particular property, she has 207 suites and three meeting rooms for which she is responsible.

How LeAnne Coury Got Started

"Right out of high school I worked for the Chamber of Commerce in the convention and sales department. That's where I first got into the convention end of the industry. I got to see how they booked the whole city, how they went after major conventions. I worked with booking blocks of hotel rooms city-wide versus working in one specific hotel.

"After about a year there, I realized I wouldn't have a chance for advancement. Hotels offer better opportunities and more money. The experience I got with the Chamber of Commerce translated well into hotel work.

"I took a position as a sales and catering secretary at the Red Lion Hotel in Oregon. Red Lion had about seventy-five very upscale hotels. I was there only six months and learned everything I could. Then I applied for a position in another hotel that I saw was under construction about two hours away. I sat with the general manager in the coffee shop for an hour or so. He ended up calling me and offering me the sales and convention manager position. It was on a trial basis because of my age; I was only twenty at the time. The drinking age was twenty-one, so they had legal issues to deal with about my selling liquor. That was a great job. They could seat a thousand people, and I pretty much ran all of that. I stayed there for three and a half years, but then an opportunity came up for me to go back to Red Lion as the sales and catering manager. It turned out to be a good move for me—more money, more knowledge. After three years I moved south, to Alabama, but there weren't as many hotel opportunities there for me, so I went into the legal field for a while and worked as a legal secretary.

"But I missed the hotels. It's usually something you either love or hate; there's no in between. I finally found a job in Mobile and traveled among five different states, promoting the hotel.

"In 1990 I started at the Quality Suites Hotel in Deerfield Beach, Florida. My first position was as sales and catering manager, and later I moved up to my current position, assistant director of sales. The next step up for me would be as director of sales, then I could even think about moving into a general manager position. The opportunities are there, and the company is willing to train you."

LeAnne Coury—on the Job

"Every day is different, unlike some jobs where the work can get monotonous. The hotel industry isn't like that. You might come in in the morning with a plan to work on a specific task, then something comes up and you end up doing something else. The meeting planners for a large group convention might come in and want to discuss details with you, so you put your other work on hold for a while.

"Basically, the way it works in the sales end of things is that you're out looking for new business and staying on top of your current business. We look for corporate customers and we want to stay in touch on a regular basis.

"You're on the phone a lot, checking details, taking care of rooming lists. There are always a lot of details, and you have to follow through on promises you make. For example, if you promised to hold ten two-bedded suites for them, you have to make sure that's what got booked, not ten king suites. And with conferences, you need to follow up on AV equipment or registration tables, that sort of thing.

"I'm up and down a lot, too; I'm not just always sitting at a desk. I walk around the hotel, double check on my groups, make sure they're happy.

"As I said, every day is new because you're working with different people all the time. That's what I think makes it fun.

"But, as with any job, there are always some downsides. Sometimes you get bogged down with paperwork, but if you're an organized person you should be able to stay on top of it. It's not too bad.

"Another thing in this business, a hotel never closes, so your hours won't always be the best. You could be working nights, weekends. However, I think once you put enough time in, you can move into some of the positions where you don't have such an uncertain schedule. With a smaller hotel, it's a little easier.

"But the advantages far outweigh the disadvantages. In sales you're working with some high-energy people in an up kind of atmosphere. We have bells on our desks, and when we book something we ring our bells.

"Doing sales blitzes is a lot of fun, too. We do ours with a theme. The most recent one was called 'We're Fishin' for Your Business.' We had special shirts with fish printed on them, as well as our logo. We also put together what we call a 'blitz bag.' They're plastic bags that we stuff with all sorts of promotional items, such as coasters, rulers, calculators. Then, unannounced, we go out and visit big office buildings. We just walk in and tell them we'd like to be able to work with them, that we're 'fishin' for their business.' We recently hit about three or four hundred businesses in this area. It's a good way to get leads and get your name out there.

"We laugh and have a good time at our job. It's fun to go to work. I've never gotten up in the morning and dreaded going in."

Advice from LeAnne Coury

"If you're going to be in this industry, you have to be a people person and have a happy personality. You always have to be able to keep a smile on your face, and if a guest or a customer is dissatisfied, you have to be able to handle it. You don't ever want to lose business.

"You have to be a team player, too. If the restaurant gets busy, for example, I'll go over and help them out there. If someone needs help, then that's what you do. Our job descriptions aren't rigidly set. But it's fun to do something different once in a while.

"When you're looking for work, you'll probably be better off working for a hotel that is corporate owned rather than a family-owned franchise. There'll be more opportunities for you to move up and probably better salaries.

"But don't get discouraged when you're starting out at the bottom. For example, a position at the front desk might not be the highest-paying job, but it's a good way to learn."

Meet Missy Soleau—
Food and Beverage Manager

In just five years, Missy Soleau worked her way up the ladder from busgirl to a position as food and beverage manager at the Quality Suites Hotel. She and LeAnne Coury, who is featured in the previous interview, work at the same property.

How Missy Soleau Got Started

"I had been in the retail business since I was sixteen, but decided I'd like to try the hotel and restaurant field. I started four or five years ago as a busgirl. I just walked into a hotel's restaurant and applied for a job. About a month later I became a waitress.

"After Hurricane Andrew, I lost my job because the hotel had structural damage. I heard that the Quality Suites was hiring and I started here as a hostess in August 1992. I worked closely with the food and beverage manager; he needed some help because the hurricane had filled the hotel. Then I was promoted to assistant food and beverage manager, and in December of 1994, when the manager left, I moved into his position.

"After high school I went to a small trade school and received my associate's degree in business administration and travel and tourism in 1990. My original plan was to work in the travel industry. But rather than sitting behind a desk taking reservations, I realized I'd prefer working directly with the people. I'm more of a people person than a phone person. It just so happened that I got a job at a hotel restaurant, and it's worked out really well. I know now I prefer working in a hotel rather than in just a restaurant.

"People here are on vacation and they really want to be catered to. Their needs are different from people who live in the area and are just going out to dinner. A lot of them are here for long periods of time, especially during the season, so you get to know them on a more personal basis. Working in a restaurant, you'd just see them that one night."

Missy Soleau—on the Job

"I do a hundred different things and wear a lot of different hats. I'm responsible for all the scheduling of the kitchen staff, all the ordering and purchasing of the food and other supplies. And because it's such a small property, I'm also responsible for the banquet end of things. I do the bookings, the setups, and the cleanups.

"No day is ever the same. I could be serving coffee in the morning, then participating in an executive meeting in the afternoon. And it could be that I'm here from 5:30 in the morning to 11:00 at night, if need be. I like to get here early in the morning, so if I do have a banquet or another event scheduled I can see that everything is going as planned. The meeting might run until five, then I have to clean up and then get the room ready for another meeting that might start at 6:00. I do have a little bit of help here, but most of the time I do it by myself. Because of the small staff, there's a lot of moving and lifting. The tables are heavy. I work six days a week, anywhere from fifty to sixty hours a week. I enjoy it—it keeps me out of trouble.

"I'm paid on a salary basis, no overtime, but if I take a day off I'm not docked. I started as an assistant food and beverage manager at an hourly wage, about $6.50. I was determined, though. Now, it figures out to about $22,800 a year, plus gratuities from the banquets.

"It's below what it should be, but the experience is what I'm looking for. All my training is on the job. This company is growing—we just purchased our fiftieth hotel (although there are hundreds, maybe thousands of franchised Quality Suites across the country)—so I can stay with the company but move to a bigger hotel. I'm flexible and able to move anywhere. If I did go to a larger hotel, I'd probably start back as assistant manager again, but the salary would probably be more than I'm earning now.

"It's very challenging work and varied. I've been here three years, and the same people come back and I really enjoy seeing them every year and catching up with them."

Advice from Missy Soleau

"I have no formal training in food and beverage, but I would recommend that anyone wanting to go into this field should go to school and get a degree. Hands-on training is the best thing, I think, but in the long run, formal training can really make a difference.

"Another thing I would like to do is go to chef school. Even if you don't plan to work full-time as a chef, it's a good skill to have. As food and beverage manager, you might have to step in and take over if your chef is out unexpectedly. And also, if you understand what's involved for a cook, you can share ideas and work better together.

"Be prepared to start off at a low salary. Eventually you'll be able to work your way up."

Salaries for Hotel Managers

Salaries for hotel managers vary greatly according to their responsibilities and the size of the hotel in which they work. In 1995, annual salaries of assistant hotel managers averaged an estimated $40,000, based on a hospitality industry survey conducted by Roth Young. According to another survey, assistants employed in large hotels with over 350 rooms averaged nearly $40,400 in 1995, while those in small hotels with no more than 150 rooms averaged more than $29,000.

Salaries of assistant managers also vary because of differences in duties and responsibilities. For example, food and beverage managers averaged an estimated $44,400, whereas front office managers averaged $30,000. The manager's level of experience is also an important factor. In 1995, salaries of general managers averaged nearly $57,000, ranging from an average of about $41,000 in hotels and motels with no more than 150 rooms to an average of about $81,000 in large hotels with over 350 rooms. Managers may earn bonuses ranging up to 15 percent of their basic salary in some hotels. In addition, they and their families may be furnished with lodging, meals, parking, laundry, and other services.

Most managers and assistants receive three to eleven paid holidays a year, paid vacation, sick leave, life insurance, medical benefits, and pension plans. Some hotels offer profit-sharing plans, educational assistance, and other benefits to their employees.

CHAPTER EIGHT

Health Services Managers

H
ealth care is a business, albeit a special one. Like every other business, it needs good management to keep it running smoothly. The term *health services manager* encompasses individuals in many different positions who plan, organize, coordinate, and supervise the delivery of health care. Health services managers include both generalists, the administrators managing or helping to manage an entire facility, and health specialists, the managers in charge of specific clinical departments or services that are found only in the health industry.

The top administrator or chief executive officer (CEO) and the assistant administrators without specific titles are health care generalists. They set the overall direction of the facilities they manage. They also are concerned with community outreach, planning, policy making, and complying with government agencies and regulations. Their range of knowledge is necessarily broad, including developments in the clinical departments as well as in the business arena. They often speak before civic groups, promote public participation in health programs, and coordinate the activities of their organizations with those of government or community agencies. CEOs make long-term institutional plans by assessing the need for services, personnel, facilities, and equipment and by recommending changes such as opening a home health service.

CEOs need leadership ability as well as technical skills to provide quality health care while, at the same time, satisfying demand for financial viability, cost containment, and public and professional accountability.

CEOs prepare for oversight and scrutiny of their facilities' past performance and plans by consumer groups, government agencies, professional oversight bodies, and insurance companies and other third-party payers.

Larger facilities typically have several assistant administrators to aid the top administrator and to handle day-to-day decisions. They may direct activities in clinical areas such as nursing, surgery, therapy, food service, and medical records; or they may oversee the activities in nonhealth areas such as finance, housekeeping, human resources, and information management.

In smaller facilities, top administrators may handle more of the details of day-to-day operations. For example, many nursing home administrators directly manage personnel, finance, operations, and admissions.

Clinical managers have more narrowly defined responsibilities than the generalists to whom they report, and they have training and/or experience in the particular field. For example, directors of physical therapy are experienced physical therapists, and most medical records administrators have bachelor's degrees in medical records administration. These managers establish and implement policies, objectives, and procedures for their departments; they evaluate personnel and work; they develop reports and budgets; and they coordinate activities with other managers.

In group practices, managers work closely with the physician owners. While an office manager may handle business affairs in small medical groups, leaving policy decisions to the physicians themselves, larger groups generally employ a full-time administrator to advise on business strategies and coordinate day-to-day business.

A small group of ten or fifteen physicians might employ a single administrator to oversee personnel matters, billing and collection, budgeting, planning, equipment outlays, and patient flow. A large practice of forty or fifty physicians may have a chief administrator and several assistants, each responsible for different areas.

Health services managers in health maintenance organizations (HMOs) perform functions similar to those in large group practices, except their staffs may be larger. The size of the administrative staff in HMOs may vary according to the type of HMO and the size of the enrolled population.

Some health services managers oversee the activities of a number of facilities in multifacility health organizations.

Health Services Managers on the Job

Many health services managers work long hours. Facilities such as nursing homes and hospitals operate around the clock, and administrators and managers may be called at all hours to deal with problems. The job also may include travel to attend meetings or to inspect satellite facilities.

Employment Figures

Health services managers held about 315,000 jobs in 1994. More than one-half of all jobs were in hospitals. About one in seven jobs were in nursing and personal care facilities, and one in eight were in offices and clinics of physicians. The remainder worked in home health agencies, medical and dental laboratories, offices of dentists and other practitioners, and other health and allied services.

Training for Health Services Managers

Health services managers must be familiar with management principles and practices. Some learn from work experience, but formal education is usually necessary for advancement. For most CEO positions, a graduate degree in health services administration, nursing administration, or business administration is required. For some generalist positions, employers seek applicants with clinical experience (as nurses or therapists, for example) as well as academic preparation in business or health services administration.

Bachelor's, master's, and doctoral degree programs in health administration are offered by colleges, universities, and schools of public health, medicine, allied health, public administration, and business administration. There are also some certificate or diploma programs, generally lasting less than one year, in health services administration and in medical office management. A master's degree in hospital administration, health services administration, long-term care administration, health sciences, public health, public administration, or business administration is regarded as the standard credential for most generalist positions in this field.

However, bachelor's degrees are adequate for some entry-level positions and a few top positions in smaller operations, and for some middle management jobs in larger ones. Bachelor's degrees may not be needed in smaller nursing homes, physician's offices, and other facilities. Appropriate experience or certificates and diplomas are sometimes acceptable. For clinical department heads, degrees in appropriate fields and work experience are usually sufficient, but courses in health services administration are helpful.

In 1995, sixty-nine schools offered accredited programs leading to master's degrees in health services administration, according to the Accrediting Commission on Education for Health Services Administration. Some graduate programs seek students with undergraduate degrees in business or health administration; however, many programs prefer students with liberal arts or health professions backgrounds. Competition for entry to these programs is keen, and applicants need above-average grades to gain admission. The programs generally last between two and three years. They include up to one year of supervised administrative experience and course work in areas such as hospital organization and management, accounting and budgeting, human resources administration, strategic planning, health economics, and health information systems.

Students generally specialize in one type of facility: hospitals, nursing homes, mental health facilities, HMOs, or outpatient care facilities, including medical groups.

New graduates with master's degrees in health services or hospital administration may start as assistant hospital administrators, or as managers of nonhealth departments, such as finance. Postgraduate residencies and fellowships are offered by hospitals and other health facilities; these are normally staff jobs. Graduates from master's degree programs also take jobs in HMOs, large group medical practices, clinics, mental health facilities, and multifacility nursing home corporations.

New recipients of bachelor's degrees in health administration usually begin as administrative assistants or assistant department heads in larger hospitals, or as department heads or assistant administrators in small hospitals or in nursing homes. Ph.D. degrees may be required to teach, consult, or do research. Nursing service administrators are usually chosen from among supervisory registered nurses with administrative abilities and advanced education.

All states and the District of Columbia require nursing home administrators to pass a licensing examination, complete a state-approved training program, and pursue continuing education. Most states also have additional requirements. A license is not required in other areas of health services management.

The Qualities You'll Need

Health services managers are often responsible for hundreds of employees and millions of dollars in facilities and equipment. To make effective decisions, they need to be open to different opinions and good at analyzing contradictory information. To motivate others to implement their decisions, they need strong leadership qualities. Tact, diplomacy, and communication skills are essential.

Looking Ahead

Health services managers advance by moving into more responsible and higher-paying positions such as assistant or associate administrator and, finally, CEO, or by moving to larger facilities.

Employment of health services managers is expected to grow much faster than the average for all occupations through the year 2005 as health services continue to expand and diversify. Hospitals will continue to employ the most managers, although the number of jobs will not be growing as fast as in other health services areas.

Employment in home health agencies and nursing and long-term care facilities will grow the fastest, due to an increased number of elderly who will need care. Demand in medical group practices will grow, too. As medical group practices and HMOs become larger and more complex, more job opportunities for department heads should emerge.

Health services managers in hospitals will face very keen competition for upper-level management jobs, a reflection of the pyramidal management structure characteristic of most large organizations. In nursing homes and other long-term care facilities, job opportunities for individuals with strong business and management skills will continue to be good.

What It's Really Like

Meet Julie Benthal— Vice President of Nursing

Julie Benthal has been a nurse for close to forty-five years. For the last few years she has been the top nursing administrator at a community hospital in Boca Raton, Florida.

How Julie Benthal Got Started

"I just wanted to care for patients. If I had been born a little later I probably would have gone to medical school, but back then becoming a doctor was not an easy route for women to take. Before becoming the vice president of nursing, I worked in critical care for years taking care of very ill patients. I loved it.

"I started accumulating administrative experience when I was a student nurse. I worked as a charge nurse then, and over the years I moved up through the ranks, from nurse manager to where I am now."

Julie Benthal—on the Job

"I'm responsible for nursing throughout the hospital. I attend all sorts of meetings and I'm on long-range planning and budget committees. It's a way of communicating and knowing what's going on in the hospital. For example, I meet with all the nurse managers once a month. We look at how we can ensure the best possible patient care and try to resolve any ongoing concerns.

"In addition to overseeing staffing and schedules, I'm also responsible for a hefty $20 million budget for the division of nursing. And I'm on the advisory board for student nurses. It's busy, but I enjoy it.

"You can work with the nursing profession and see it grow and develop. With health reform, a lot of creative innovation is going on right now. Hospitals and staffs are being reorganized to better meet the needs of the patients. It's called patient-centered care.

"People are rethinking the way they work—not in just nursing, but in all the departments. It's a much more collaborative team effort. The idea of health reform is to give better care that is less costly.

"I also find it rewarding that I get a chance to network a lot and share ideas and information. There's a lot of flexibility and a lot of challenge. It's never boring.

"What I don't like is fighting for more staff. That's a problem that comes up once a year when we're dealing with budgets."

Advice from Julie Benthal

"Make sure you get several years of hands-on experience before you consider administration. And be prepared to get the right education and training. You'll have to have a master's degree in addition to your B.S.N."

Meet Laurie DeJong—Assistant Director, Physical Therapy

Laurie DeJong is assistant director of physical therapy at a large community hospital in South Florida. She graduated in 1984 with a bachelor's degree in physical therapy from Quinnipiac College in Hamden, Connecticut.

How Laurie DeJong Got Started

"I spent four years working in a rehab hospital, and while there I started doing pediatrics and spent two years working with children as well as adults on an outpatient basis.

"For one year I had my own private practice doing home health and consultation in schools. I then moved to another state and joined the hospital as a staff physical therapist.

"I always liked medical things. I started playing hospital when I was about two. My parents told me I couldn't be a nurse, but I could become a doctor if I wanted to. But when I was seventeen I realized how long it would take me to become a doctor. I learned about physical therapy from a guidance counselor, then realized that it would be the right career for me."

Laurie DeJong—on the Job

"Physical therapists generally specialize, working in a particular setting or with certain kinds of patients. We evaluate patients, looking for pain, their flexibility or range of motion, their strength, and what kind of functional activities they do or need to do. For example, if the patient is a dancer, she needs to dance; if it's a child, she needs to play, if it's an adult, she needs to work, and so on. We do a complete evaluation, sitting down and talking to the patient about what the patient is looking for, about what we're looking for, and then, depending upon the person and her needs, we would design an appropriate treatment plan.

"Treatment plans generally include manual therapy, doing stretching or strengthening exercises, or specific joint mobilization exercises. We also use modalities such as hot packs, cold packs, ultrasound, or electric stimulation to help reduce pain.

"We do a lot of teaching, too, explaining the exercises to the patients, so they can carry on the activities at home without us. We do a lot of education in terms of posture and how patients can prevent their injuries from recurring. If our patients are children, we also work with the parents or teachers, explaining how to do the exercises or how best to help the child function in the school arena. On the sports field we may be educating the coaches as to what kind of exercises a specific child needs. We also run classes, such as back schools, body awareness, or risk management, within the hospital and within industry.

"Part of the job is doing documentation—that's the part most of us don't like, but it's necessary.

"But it's a great profession to have. You can specialize in so many different areas. We all come out with a basic background, and then you can tailor your expertise to the area you prefer.

"In my job I like the fact that I can do a lot of different things. We have a lot of hands-on time with our patients. We develop a treatment plan and then we see the patients generally two or three times a week for at least a month. I like working with the kids because I can see them for years. A child with developmental delays, such as cerebral palsy, for example, I'll see forever. We get to develop a rapport, spending time one-on-one with our patients. Doctor's don't have the time to do that.

"I also like being able to keep up with the changes in health care, keeping myself on the cutting edge of what's happening out there.

"The stresses are the same as for everyone else. There's not enough time to do the job you have to do. It's also a challenge with the changes that are happening in health care. Some of the changes aren't fun, and we don't like what's happening. There are now insurance companies telling us how we should treat our patients, as opposed to our dictating the kind of care our patients need. You'll find patients saying they know they need more treatment, but they won't be coming back to you because they can't afford it."

Advice from Laurie DeJong

"You have to really love working with people and you have to possess a great deal of patience. Change and improvement don't happen overnight. Often the person you're working with is impatient to get better, but you have to be the steadying force."

Salaries for Health Services Managers

Earnings vary by type and size of the facility, as well as by level of responsibility. For example, the Medical Group Management Association reported that the median salary for administrators in small group practices with net revenues of $2 million or less was $46,600; for those in very large group practices with net revenues over $50 million, it was $166,700.

According to a survey by *Modern Healthcare* magazine, half of all hospital CEOs earned $165,500 or more in 1995.

Salaries varied according to size of facility and geographic region. Clinical department heads' salaries varied too. Median total compensation in 1995 for heads of the following clinical departments were:

Ambulatory/outpatient services	$62,400
Home health	$55,000
Imaging/radiology	$58,000
Nursing services	$88,000
Physical therapy	$58,200
Rehabilitation services	$66,700

According to a survey sponsored by the American Health Care Association, nursing home administrators had median annual total compensation of $47,400 in 1994. Executives often receive bonuses based on performance outcomes such as cost-containment, quality assurance, and patient satisfaction.

Professional Associations

Chapter One: Examining the Options

For a wide variety of information on general managers and top executives, including educational programs and job listings, contact:

American Management Association
Management Information Service
135 West 50th Street
New York, NY 10020

National Management Association
2210 Arbor Boulevard
Dayton, OH 45439

Chapter Two: Government Bigwigs

For more information on careers in public administration, consult your elected representatives and local library.

Information on state governments can be obtained from:

Council of State Governments
P.O. Box 11910
Iron Works Pike
Lexington, KY 40578

Information on appointed officials in local government can be obtained from:

International City/County Management Association
777 North Capitol Street NE, Suite 500
Washington, DC 20002

Chapter Three: Education Administrators

For information on elementary and secondary school principals, assistant principals, and central office administrators, contact:

American Federation of School Administrators
1729 21st Street NW
Washington, DC 20009

American Association of School Administrators
1801 North Moore Street
Arlington, VA 22209

For information on elementary school principals and assistant principals, contact:

National Association of Elementary School Principals
1615 Duke Street
Alexandria, VA 22314-3483

For information on secondary school principals and assistant principals, contact:

National Association of Secondary School Principals
1904 Association Drive
Reston, VA 22091

For information on college student affairs administrators, contact:

National Association of Student Personnel Administrators
1875 Connecticut Avenue NW, Suite 418
Washington, DC 20009-5728

For information on collegiate registrars and admissions officers, contact:

American Association of Collegiate
Registrars and Admissions Officers
One Dupont Circle NW, Suite 330
Washington, DC 20036-1171

Chapter Four: Financial Managers

For information about financial management careers, contact:

Financial Management Association, International
College of Business Administration
University of South Florida
Tampa, FL 33620-5500

Financial Managers Society
8 South Michigan Avenue, Suite 500
Chicago, IL 60603

For information about financial management careers in banking and related financial institutions, contact:

American Bankers Association
Center for Banking Information
1120 Connecticut Avenue NW
Washington, DC 20036

For information about financial management careers in credit unions, contact:

Credit Union Executives Society
P.O. Box 14167
Madison, WI 53714

For information about financial careers in business credit management, the Certified Credit Executive program, and institutions offering graduate courses in credit and financial management, contact:

National Association of Credit Management (NACM)
8815 Centre Park Drive
Columbia, MD 21045-2117

For information about careers in corporate cash management and the Certified Cash Manager program, contact:

Treasury Management Association
7315 Wisconsin Avenue
Bethesda, MD 20814

For information about the Chartered Financial Analyst program, contact:

Association for Investment Management and Research
5 Boar's Head Lane
P.O. Box 3668
Charlottesville, VA 22903

For information about financial management careers in the health care industry, contact:

Healthcare Financial Management Association
2 Westbrook Corporate Center, Suite 700
Westchester, IL 60154

For information on careers and courses for financial managers in the banking industry, contact:

Savings and Community Bankers of America
Education Services
Center For Financial Studies
200 Barlow Road
Fairfield, CT 06430

Information about careers with the Federal Reserve System is available from the human resources department of the Federal Reserve bank serving each geographic area or from:

Board of Governors
The Federal Reserve System
Division of Human Resources Management
Washington, DC 20551

State bankers' associations can furnish specific information about job opportunities in their states. Or write directly to a particular bank to inquire about job openings. For the names and addresses of banks and savings and related institutions, as well as the names of their principal officers, consult one of the following directories:

The American Financial Directory (Norcross, GA: McFadden Business Publications)

The U.S. Savings and Loan Directory (Chicago: Rand McNally & Co.)

Rand McNally Credit Union Directory (Chicago: Rand McNally & Co.)

Polk's World Bank Directory (Nashville: R.L. Polk & Co.)

Chapter Five: Marketing and Sales Managers

For information about careers in sales and marketing management, contact:

American Marketing Association
250 South Wacker Drive
Chicago, IL 60606

Sales and Marketing Executives International
458 Statler Office Tower
Cleveland, OH 44115

For information about careers in advertising management, contact:

American Advertising Federation
Education Services Department
1101 Vermont Avenue NW, Suite 500
Washington, DC 20005

Information about careers in promotion management is available from:

Council of Sales Promotion Agencies
750 Summer Street
Stamford, CT 06901

Promotion Marketing Association of America, Inc.
322 Eighth Avenue, Suite 1201
New York, NY 10001

Information about careers in public relations management is available from:

Public Relations Society of America
33 Irving Place
New York, NY 10003-2376

Chapter Six: Engineering Managers

High school students interested in obtaining general information on a variety of engineering disciplines should contact the Junior Engineering Technical Society by sending a self-addressed business-size envelope affixed with six first-class stamps to:

JETS-Guidance
1420 King Street, Suite 405
Alexandria, VA 22314

Non-high schoolers and those wanting more information should contact societies representing the individual branches of engineering. Each can provide information about careers in the particular branch. These addresses are listed in the *Occupational Outlook Handbook*, available at your library, and *On the Job: Real People Working in Engineering*, by Blythe Camenson (NTC/Contemporary Publishing), which provides detailed information about engineering careers.

Chapter Seven: Restaurant and Hotel Managers

Information about careers as restaurant and food service managers, food and beverage servers, chefs, cooks, and other kitchen workers, as well as information how to obtain directories of two- and four-year college programs in restaurant and food service management and shorter courses that will prepare you for other food service careers is available from:

Educational Foundation of the National
   Restaurant Association
250 South Wacker Drive, Suite 1400
Chicago, IL 60606

Information about certification as a food service management professional is also available from the above address.
   General information on hospitality careers may be obtained
from:

Council on Hotel, Restaurant, and Institutional Education
1200 17th Street NW
Washington, DC 20036-3097

For information on the American Culinary Federation's ap-
prenticeship and certification programs for cooks, as well as a
list of accredited culinary programs, write to:

American Culinary Federation
P.O. Box 3466
St. Augustine, FL 32085

For information on careers and scholarships in hotel management, contact:

American Hotel and Motel Association (AH&MA)
Information Center
1201 New York Avenue NW
Washington, DC 20005-3931

For information on educational programs, including cor-
respondence courses, in hotel and restaurant management,
write to:

Educational Institute of AH&MA
P.O. Box 1240
East Lansing, MI 48826

For information on careers in housekeeping management, contact:

National Executive Housekeepers Association, Inc.
1001 Eastwind Drive, Suite 301
Westerville, OH 43081

For information on hospitality careers, as well as how to purchase a directory of colleges and other schools offering programs in hotel and restaurant administration, write to:

Council on Hotel, Restaurant, and Institutional Education
1200 17th Street NW
Washington, DC 20036-3097

Chapter Eight: Health Services Managers

Information about health administration is available from:

American College of Healthcare Executives
840 North Lake Shore Drive
Chicago, IL 60611

Information about undergraduate and graduate academic programs in this field is available from:

Association of University Programs in
   Health Administration
1911 North Fort Myer Drive, Suite 503
Arlington, VA 22209

For a list of accredited graduate programs in health services administration, contact:

Accrediting Commission on Education for
   Health Services Administration
1911 North Fort Myer Drive, Suite 503
Arlington, VA 22209

For information about career opportunities in long-term care administration, contact:

American College of Health Care Administrators
325 South Patrick Street
Alexandria, VA 22314

For information about career opportunities in medical group practices and ambulatory care management, contact:

Medical Group Management Association
104 Inverness Terrace East
Englewood, CO 80112-5306

About the Author

A full-time writer of career books, Blythe Camenson works hard to help job seekers make educated choices. She firmly believes that with enough information, readers can find long-term, satisfying careers. To that end, she researches traditional as well as unusual occupations, talking to a variety of professionals about what their jobs are really like. In all of her books she includes firsthand accounts from people who can reveal what to expect in each occupation.

Camenson was educated in Boston, earning her B.A. in English and psychology from the University of Massachusetts and her M.Ed. in counseling from Northeastern University.

In addition to *Careers for Born Leaders*, she has written more than two dozen books for NTC/Contemporary Publishing.